Benjamin Franklin De Costa, James McGee

Notes on the History of Fort George

During the Colonial and Revolutionary Periods

Benjamin Franklin De Costa, James McGee

Notes on the History of Fort George
During the Colonial and Revolutionary Periods

ISBN/EAN: 9783337155117

Printed in Europe, USA, Canada, Australia, Japan

Cover: Foto ©ninafisch / pixelio.de

More available books at **www.hansebooks.com**

NOTES

ON THE

History of Fort George

DURING THE

COLONIAL AND REVOLUTIONARY PERIODS,

WITH CONTEMPORANEOUS DOCUMENTS

AND AN APPENDIX.

BY B. F. DeCOSTA,

AUTHOR OF "LAKE GEORGE: ITS SCENES AND CHARACTERISTICS," &C., &C.

Embosomed amid its green hills . . . and alone in its picturesque beauty, spreads, sparkling to the day, the picturesque Lake George, with its hundred islands and their silent woods. Here, exhaustless as those pure waters, the poet, the novelist, the sober historian, or the excursive dramatist, may find by the cottage fireside, materials for their respective purposes.—BRYANT.

New York:
J. SABIN & SONS, 84 NASSAU STREET.
LONDON: 22 BUCKINGHAM STREET.
1871.

PREFACE.

HE fragments embodied in the following sketch were, for the greater part, accumulated by the writer while engaged in preparing a popular work on Lake George. They are now given in a separate and permanent form, not as constituting anything like a complete history, but rather as interesting materials affording some fresh illustration of the annals of one of the most beautiful and celebrated localities in our land.

These gleanings have come from every source accessible to the compiler, and include nearly everything of interest that he has found in connection with the history of Fort George. Many of the documents thus embodied appear in print for the first time, being transcripts from the original MSS. It will be a subject of gratulation if this publication stimulates fresh, and successful, search for additional material.

NEW YORK, 1871.

NOTES

ON THE

History of Fort George.

CHAPTER I.

IN THE EARLY TIMES, the waters of Lake George owed their importance to the fact that they formed a part of a great route of communication between New York and Montreal. In pursuing this route, the traveller could pass nearly the whole distance between these two points in boats and canoes. Hence the many struggles of the French and English, and, later, the English and the Americans, for the possession of this route.*

Born of the clouds, and cradled among the overhanging hills, Lake George sleeps almost as tranquil as a sea of glass, the ideal of loveliness

---

* To help out a theory, it has been stated that the route by Lake St. Sacrament was the exclusive route in early times. The truth, however, appears from the following: "The Route from Montreal to Albany is begun by ferrying over to *la Praire*, and thence a Land Carriage, over low, wet Ground, fifteen Miles to St. *Jean*. From this Port, which is truly but a Magazine, they go in a Schooner to Crown Point, a very considerable Fortress, at the Head of Lake Champlain, and the Mouth of Wood Creek. Two Ways lead from hence towards Hudson's River; the one by Lake St. Sacrament, in which there is a Mile Portage, in the Streight between the Lake and Wood Creek. 'Tis very dangerous passing this Lake at the Change of Weather, by Reason of the great Waves arising without much Wind, and the inaccessible Cliffs of vast high Mountains on the East Side. At the Head, the Lake divides into two Bays, from the Eastermost of which is a Portage twelve Miles, or more, to Hudson's River. And from this Portage to Albany, you go down Hudson's River, without any other Interruption than two little Portages of about Half a Mile each. The other Way from Crown Point towards Hudson's River, is altogether by Wood Creek, and you are only interrupted with a Portage of a Stone's Throw or two in Length, at a Place called Kingiaguaghtenec. The Portage from Wood to Hudson's River is twelve Miles also; and the Passage thence to Albany is by the same River, and with the same Interruption. The whole performed in five or six Days."—LEWIS EVANS' "Essays," etc., pp. 19.

and peace. First seen and named by a white man in 1646,* it retained its original appropriate appellation—Lake St. Sacrament†—until 1755, when it witnessed the first pitched battle, and, through the victory of the English, lost the only name worthy of its beauty and renown. Previous to this year, however, General Johnson had visited the lake. In 1746, just one hundred years after its discovery by Jogues, he went thither with various Indian tribes, who put up their symbols, or *totems*, to "alarm the French;" still no action took place.

But, in 1755, the bold aggressions of the French had caused much apprehension, and the home government, in connection with the colonists, resolved to force the intruders from the advanced positions everywhere assumed, and especially from Ticonderoga, at which place they had established a fortress and planted the French flag. An army was accordingly assembled, under General William Johnson, at the head, or south end of Lake George; but before he could move against Ticonderoga and Crown Point, the French, led by General Dieskau, on the 28th of August, attacked him in his camp, when Johnson fought the Battle of Lake George, and, by the aid of skillful officers, gained his well-known victory, for which he was knighted, finding, at the same time, great popularity among all the people.‡ The story of this battle has so often been told, that it is only necessary, for our present purpose, to observe that, at the close of this memorable summer day, the French, near Bloody Pond, received the last blow at the hands of the English, and fled in confusion to Ticonderoga.§

---

* May 29, 1646, Isaac Jogues, S. J. and Jean Bourdon, the engineer, were on their way from Montreal to the Mohawk region to perfect a treaty with the Indians; and on the eve of this day, the festival of *Corpus Christi*, they reached the lake, and named it "Lake of the Blessed Sacrament" (*Lac du St. Sacrement*).

† Poets and others fable that the name was given in commemoration of the purity of its water, yet the Jesuit is particular to state that it was in honor of the festival. *See* "Relations des Jesuites," 1646, p. 15. It may also be noticed here that Champlain, in 1609, saw the falls at the outlet of the lake, but there is nothing to indicate that he ever saw the lake itself; he knew it only through the accounts of the Indians. That Jogues saw the lake prior to 1646 is a mere fancy, unsupported by due evidence.

‡ The credit of this victory, nevertheless, belonged to Gen. Wyman, who assumed command early in the day, when Johnson was wounded and carried from the field.

§ The following is an additional item of interest recently contributed to the history of this battle: "Our Cannon (which under God it appears to me) saved us were heard down as low as near Saratoga, notwithstanding the wind was in the south, & something considerable, & which by the way was a great disadvantage to our troops, as the smoke was drove in our faces. The wounded was brought in very fast, & it was with the utmost difficulty that their wounds could be dressed fast enough, even in the most superficial manner, having in about three hours near forty men to be dressed, & Dr. PYNCHON, his mate & Billy (one of his students) & myself were all to do it, my mate being at Fort Lyman attending upon divers sick men there. The bullets flew like hail-stones about our ears all the time of dressing, as we had not a place prepared of safety, to dress in the wounded in, but through God's goodness we received no hurt any more than the bark of the trees & chips flying in our faces by accidental shots, which were something frequent. Our Tent was shot through in diver places, which we thought best to leave and retire a few rods behind a shelter of a log house, which so loose laid as to let the balls through very often. I have not time to give a list of the dead which are many, by reason I have not time to attend the wounded as they ought to be."—The Campaigns against Crown Point in 1755 and 1756. Correspondence of Dr. Thos. Williams. "Historical Magazine," New Series, Vol. VII, No. IV, April, 1870.

Nevertheless, General Johnson failed to follow up his advantage, and interested himself with building a fort on the bank of the lake. This fort he named "Fort William Henry,"* and, at the same time, he caused the name of the lake to be changed to Lake George,† in honor of the reigning sovereign of England.

Having finished the fort, General Johnson retired, leaving a small garrison to hold the place. Quite a number of old powder-horns are still in existence, which show, in their rude carvings (the work of soldiers during idle hours), the plan and appearance of the fort, which, in the official reports, is depicted with scientific accuracy.

From the inquiry into the military conduct of General Shirley, then having the general command of the British forces in America, we learn that, on Nov. 4, 1755, he was at Albany, devising a winter expedition against Ticonderoga and Crown Point; but nothing was done, for the reason, it is averred, that the ice was too thin. ("Inquiry," p. 53).

On following year, the weak and inefficient Earl of Loudon assumed the military command in North America, but nothing was eventually done, and the time was filled up with inconclusive skirmishes around the lake between the French and English scouts. In the same way the winter was passed; yet, in the spring of 1757, the French became more demonstrative, and, on the night of March 18th, led by Rigaud, they attempted to surprise the fort, but failed. With the advent of summer, however, the gallant Montcalm was afield, and, by August 3d, he had invested Fort William Henry, which was surrendered by the commander, Colonel Monroe, after a siege of six days, an event that might have been averted but for the dastardly conduct of Webb, the commander of Fort Edward. At this time occurred the well-known massacre of the English, the details of which event, though sufficiently shocking of themselves, have, nevertheless, been made the subject of wild exaggeration by prejudiced historical writers.

When Montcalm once more retired to the North, he left Fort William Henry a heap of smoldering ruins, which were never afterwards disturbed, as the site possessed no real advantages.

The French had now fully revenged the defeat of 1755, and were in confident possession of Ticonderoga. Accordingly, the next summer, the English moved again to dispossess them. Led by the ill-starred Abercrombie, they embarked on the lake in beautiful order, from the docks near the charred remains of Fort William Henry, and, sixteen thou-

---

* The remains of this fort may still be seen in front of the well-known "Fort William Henry Hotel," Caldwell. In the "Paris Documents," the French speak of this Fort as "Fort George," though it never was so called by the English. *See* "N. Y. Coll. Doc.," Vol. x, p. 596.

† Cooper, in one of his novels, teaches that the Indian name of the lake was "Horicon,"—*Silvery Water*—which, of course, is not the case. Parkman says: "I have seen an old Latin map on which the name 'Horicini' is set down as belonging to a neighboring tribe. This appears to be only a misprint for 'Horoconi,' that is 'Iroconi,' or 'Iroquois.' In an old English map, prefixed to the rare work, 'A Treatise of New England,' the 'Lake of the Hierocoyes is laid down.' "—" Jesuits in America," p. 219*n*. I may add, that an old Dutch map puts the country of the "Horikons" near Cape Cod.

sand strong, confidently moved to assault the French. But, after the display of a peerless valor before the walls of Ticonderoga, on July 7th the army was forced to retreat in haste to the south end of the lake, leaving behind a large number of dead and wounded. On Sunday evening, July 9th, the troops landed at Fort William Henry, broken and disheartened.

On his return to the head of the lake, Abercrombie began to send cannon and ammunition to Albany, and, at the same time, occupied his troops in the construction of intrenchments, as stated by the French and other authorities; but the extent and character of these works do not appear to be known.*

The following year a new English army was raised, and placed under the direction of General Amherst.† This commander resolved, at all hazard, to retrieve the disaster of Abercrombie. He accordingly made every preparation to drive the French from Ticonderoga, and recover the free use of the lakes.

It was in June 21, 1759, that Amherst reached Lake George with the bulk of the army designed to operate against Ticonderoga. Mante, in his account of the campaign, says:

"In the evening he encamped on the banks of Lake George, and the next day, with the assistance of Colonel Montressor,‡ the chief engineer, traced out the ground for the erection of a fort." ("History of the War in America," p. 207.)

---

* August 1, 1758. The French report that the English "occupy two islands on the lake, in each of which they have a guard of four hundred men; that Captain Rogers is out every day scouting; sometimes north, at other times, south; that they have intrenched themselves with trees; that there isn't any cannon in their intrenchments, but in the little fort." ("Coll. Doc.," Vol. x, p. 850.) The French commander also says that the "English were intending to amuse us only by seizing the islands in Lake St. Sacrament." Where was the "little fort"? Montcalm says, in a memoir on the situation: "The enemy will remain in force at Chouaguen until winter; in eight days they will have constructed there, as at the head of Lake St. Sacrament, an intrenchment impregnable to an assault of five thousand men, of whatever description. (*Ibid*, p. 871.) Possibly one of the places fortified at this time was Recluse Island, where there are still to be seen the remains of earth-works.

† Jeffrey Amherst was of Kentish descent, born at Riverhead, England, Jan. 20, 1717. He was an ensign at fourteen, and, at twenty-five, aid-de-camp to Lord Ligonier. In 1756 he commanded a regiment, and in 1758 he was appointed to service in America, with the rank of major-general. He commanded at the capture of Louisburg, and afterwards succeeded Abercrombie as commander in America. After the peace he returned to London. In 1763 he became Governor of Guernsey, and afterward took a seat in the Privy Council. Advanced to the peerage, he served as commander-in-chief of the British forces. In 1795 he was superseded in his command by the Duke of York, for which he was compensated by an earldom, and the title of field-marshal. He died August 3, 1797, aged eighty-one years.

‡ "James Montresor became Director of Engineers and Lieutenant-Colonel in the British Army 4th January, 1758, in which year he was at the head of the Engineer Department, in the expedition against Ticonderoga, under Abercrombie. He drew the plan of Fort Stanwix and the surrounding country in the summer of the same year. *New-York Documentary History*, 8vo, IV, 425. He was Chief Engineer also to Amherst's Expedition, and superintended the construction of the Fort at the head of Lake George, in July, 1759. *Knox's Journal*, I, 403. He obtained in 1771 a grant of 10,000 acres of land at the Forks of the Pagkatagkan or Otter Creek, in the present town of Panton, Vt., and in May, 1772, became Colonel in the army. He died in December, 1775. *Army Lists; New-York Land Papers*." ("N. Y. Coll. Doc.," Vol. x, p. 911.)

The fort thus planned was Fort George, which, though never finished, has always maintained a prominent place in the recollections of the people, and often figured in connection with important historical events from that time down to the close of the Revolution. Since that period it has been the subject of neglect and decay.

The fort was laid out on the brow of a low rocky hill, and was situated about five or six hundred yards from the border of the lake. The situation was one of no strength, being easily commanded from all the neighboring heights; yet, perhaps, with the means and men at command, they could hardly have done much better at that time.

For the best published plan of the work, we are indebted to a woman, Mary Ann Rocque, "Topographer to His Royal Highness the Duke of Gloucester," who, in 1765, published at London "A Set of Plans and Forts in America, reduced from Actual Surveys." Sketch fourteen of this work shows the general plan of Fort George, and indicates the portion actually finished, which consisted of the south-west bastion. Its ruins may be seen to-day.

In this plan a temporary stockade, with two guns, is shown at the north, a little more than half way to the lake; while the quarters of the officers and men, together with the magazine and storehouse, are also delineated. The author of the sketch states that, at this time, there was a saw-mill in the swamp or low land to the south-west of the fort. On the north-east an octagonal space appears to have been devoted to a kitchen-garden, while a rude stone wall extended from the stockade in a curved line running north-east and south-west to the vicinity of the fort. The remains of this wall, which appears to have covered the front of the encampment, may still be traced for a considerable distance.*
The left wing of the troops appears to have rested on the lake.

In the journal of a Massachusetts soldier connected with Amherst's army, the eminence upon which the fort is situated is called "Element Hill," though the name does not occur elsewhere. The situation is one of great beauty, and commands a fine view of the lake.

The march of Amherst to the lake is best described by Samuel Warner, one of the volunteers from Wilbraham, Massachusetts. As will be perceived, his sketch is very rude in its orthography, and could be bettered in other respects, yet he nevertheless gives a vivid idea of the fatigues endured on the day in question. Warner writes in his journal:

"Thursday 21st this Day we marcht from fort Edward with about ten Regiments we struck our tents about brake of Day slong our packs about Run Rise and stood y^m on a full ouer then marcht forword Nor onloaded Nor Rested till we got within five miles of Lake gorge there Rested about one ouer and half varey hot men allmost Beet out By

---

* The description is limited to the following: "A. Fort showing what was finished. 1. Officer's Barracks. 2. Soldier's Barracks. 3. Powder Magazine. B. Stockaded Fort erected to serve while the other was building. Guard Room. The Kitchen. 66. Store Houses. 7. Saw Mill in swamp southwest."

going without vittuals in the morning about 500 teems and wagins the officers had no packs the general and other big officers had horsis and Servens they did not consider the poore Solders Had they Had any Compashoon upon poore Solders they wood not a dun as they Did one man Dyed By Reason of such Hard traveling and Drinking of Warter this was a Conectucut man and two or three more it was said they ware a Dying the armey was marcht of in the moring on a sudden and had not time to git any Refreshment to Carey with them But God in His providence has spared men's Lives & Carried them hather to *we shall not Dey Before our time.*" ("Wilbraham Centennial," p. 210.)

So scanty are the records of these movements, that it is necessary to resort for information to the crude, but truthful, journals of the soldiers of the day.

Under the date of July 1st and 2d, Knox says :

" Wet weather: the troops are employed in constructing a stone fortress fit to contain a garrison of six hundred men; it is of an irregular form, situated on a rock, has one front to the lake, and a large tract of morass surrounds the other faces of it; a casement is to be built in the fort, spacious enough to receive four hundred men at least; and there is a plenty of good limestone, and excellent brick and clay on the spot." ("Historical Journal," Vol. 1, p. 379.) At this time, he says, there was also "a redoubt which covers our left flank at a distance of about five hundred yards." This is probably the temporary stockade delineated in the sketch by Mary Ann Rocque;* though, by referring to the scale of this female topographer, it will appear that the distances do not agree. Mary Ann Rocque's distances are evidently miscalculated, being too small.

Quoting, again, from the journal of Warner, whose meaning, notwithstanding the style of his composition, is tolerably clear, we read, under date of Tuesday, July 3d :

" There was four Brase 18 pounders or 22 Brought in to Day Sum Small pesses the 2d Recruits from Boston and harford came in to Day—Capt Jacob with 30 Men went out to day to find the inemy if could find any 24 more was dug up out of one hole whare we did Build the fort four Iron guns 22 pounders came in and afterwards two more Brase guns in the Hole making 10 22 or 24 pounder and 12 twelve pounders." (" Wilbraham Centennial.")

---

* Some distance south-east of Fort George, and on the south side of the old military road, are the scarcely distinguishable remains of an earth-work, or redoubt, known as " Fort Gage." The author, with the most careful inquiry, has never been able to ascertain its origin, though it figured in a colonial story, published in the "Knickerbocker Magazine." It is evidently of about the same age as Fort George. In 1812, there was still some portion of the woodwork remaining, though it has now disappeared. It is quite curious, on the whole, that the residents in this vicinity are able to give no clear tradition in connection with the fort, while they furnish so many stories on every other antiquarian topic.

The guns thus unearthed were buried by Abercrombie the previous year. Perhaps that general transported fewer guns to Albany than the French supposed.

While these operations were going on, the French ascended the lake from Ticonderoga, took possession of the adjacent islands,* and boldly attacked parties of English who were at work near the forts chopping fire-wood, the Indians even scalping a number of the "Jersey Blues," and flourishing their bloody trophies in sight of the English lines.† July 4th, Knox writes:

"Our engineers make great progress in erecting the new fort, and have got a fresh supply of bricklayers and masons." And, again:

"A number of men are employed in making brick and lime; others in works of various kinds, relating to further operations of the campaign, particularly at the new fort, the sloop, batteaus, &c." ("Historical Journal," p. 381-2.)

Next, for information regarding the state of affairs, we turn to the journal of Warner, which, unfortunately, is too brief:

"Thursday 5th. *** alarum At Night By Y^e Reson of an indians fiering on one of the Senterey and he Riturned a Shoot again and wonded him by the Sine of Blood there is a fort a Reacted the North end of Element Hill."

Again, we read:

"Saturday 7th I went about the Element Hill on the North End of it there is a fort of 14 squares or turns in it made with wood and Stoane the Length of about 8 Roods, the wedth about Eighteen feet from outside to outside the thickness of the Wall two feet and ½ the hith about five feet."

But Warner appears to refer to the temporary stockade, already mentioned on page 5, unless, indeed, by "Element Hill" he meant the hill on which was situated the fort now called Fort Gage, spoken of

---

* "Early this morning [July 12] a detachment of grenadiers and rangers, with a few Indians, in all about four hundred, commanded by Major Campbell, imbarked in batteaus, and proceeded to the islands on the lake to drive the enemy from thence; they were convoyed by a floating-battery of one gun, with a Sargeant and six artillery men; and the rangers and the Indians were advanced in whale-boats. About eight, the van with the light troops were fired upon, whereby a Sergeant was killed and an Indian wounded, which brought on a smart firing on both sides, until the Major ordered to cease and retire, that the Proe might come into action; accordingly she worked up and gave them a fire, which obliged the enemy to abandon their posts, and return to their canoes; the Major then endeavored to come up with them, but found it impossible, their canoes, which were made of birch bark, being lighter and easier worked than our boats, &c. We fired several shots at them, but are uncertain as to any execution. After chacing for some time, the Major went back to the islands, burnt and destroyed all their works and huts, and returned with his detachment to the camp." ("Knox's Journal.") The reference to the "Proe" is explained under date of July 7, where Knox says: "An iron eighteen pounder was mounted to-day, in the stern of a new-built *proe*, and was afterwards loaded and discharged for trial; she rolled considerably, which is imputed to her being too narrow for her length.

† *See* "N. Y. Mercury," July 9, 1759.

in the note page 6. This, however, does not appear probable. At that time, the work on Fort George went on with much rapidity. Knox writes, July 20:

"The different forts and posts between this camp and Albany are garrisoned by independent companies and provincials, all subjected to the command of Colonel Montressor, who remains here for that purpose, and to forward the new fort." ("Historical Journal," p. 396.)

We find, however, that Amherst did not wait for this fort to be finished before moving to attack the French.

July 21st, he advanced against Ticonderoga, embarking his fine army in whale-boats and batteaux, sailing in perfect quiet in four columns. But as it is no part of the author's plan to write a general history of these proceedings, it will be sufficient to observe, here, that he reached the foot of the lake without meeting any opposition from the French, who abandoned their outworks and retreated to Ticonderoga, upon which fortress Amherst opened fire with his artillery, and, on the 27th, captured the place, with a total loss of thirty or forty in killed and wounded. Thus easily did he accomplish that for which Abercrombie, with a great sacrifice of life, fought in vain.

Amherst, nevertheless, repeated the policy pursued by Sir William Johnson after the Battle of Lake George, and neglected to follow the retreating French, applying himself instead to the improvement of the fortifications.

In the meanwhile, the labor at Fort George went on, as it was the policy of Amherst to make his line of communication with Albany perfectly safe, and accomplish his work so that it might stand securely in after times.

Knox writes, at Ticonderoga, under date of July 28:

"By our last accounts from the south side of Lake George, Colonel Montressor had got the new fort in a respectable posture of defense, which is now called Fort George." ("Historical Journal," p. 403.)

But, with the completion of the bastion, the work finally ceased, and most persons appear to have forgotten that anything more was originally intended. The ultimate fall of the French power in America at last made the completion quite unnecessary; we have, therefore, little to add to the sketch of this period, as, with the discontinuance of Amherst's operations on the lake, the whole region lost its importance. Even as early as September 21, 1759, Lieutenant-Governor De Lancey issued a proclamation announcing that the few inhabitants who had previously established their abodes in the vicinity of the fort could safely return to their homes.

During the time intervening between the Colonial and the Revolutionary period, the fort appears to have attracted no attention, and was allowed to decay under the hand of time. Governor Tryon said, in 1774, that Fort Edward was wholly abandoned, and that only "a few men are kept at the works at the south end of Lake George to facilitate the transportation to the next posts, which are Ticonderoga and Crown Point." ("N. Y. Doc. Hist.," Vol. I, p. 512.) The fort was practically abandoned in 1768. At this time, Mr. Samuel Deal had built a *petti-auga*, a vessel like that in which Cornelius Vanderbilt began his career as a Staten Island ferryman, and designed to use it on the lake, "if any freight offers worth going over." This vessel was placed in charge of one John Jones, at Fort George. Mr. Deal, himself, sought to establish business at Ticonderoga. As early as 1773, Mr. Deal, who was a merchant of New York, was interested in improvements at Ticonderoga, and petitioned the government for the exclusive right to establish a ferry* over the lake. With him was associated one Lieutenant Stoughton, who was drowned in the lake near the close of 1767, when his boat went to the bottom with all its valuable freight.

Already there was quite a number of settlers within a few miles of the fort; and the Indians, likewise, resorted to the region to pursue their occupation as hunters. Frequent scenes of violence took place, as the white man questioned the Indian's rights, and, in the conflicts that ensued, the latter sometimes fell before his murderous foe.† The inhabitants were, in some instances, of a rude and lawless character, while the lives of the people generally were more or less disturbed, at this period, by the operations of reckless men on the New Hampshire Grants, who engaged in aggravating broils, and whose leaders were, at last, proclaimed felons, having a price set upon their heads.‡ Such was the general condition of the country around Fort George down to 1775, at which time, one Philip Skene, of Skenesboro', had received a commission from England that was intended to give him authority, not only as "Governor" of Ticonderoga and vicinity, but also of Fort George. Subsequent events prevented the assumption of the duties of the office, for, when the Revolution broke out, all things assumed a new aspect.

---

* July 19, 1775, Peter T. Curtenius is addressed by Jno. Burger, from Ticonderoga, who says: "I have seen the petition of Mr. John Spardin to the Provincial Congress of New York, who lives at this landing; was placed here by his Majesty King George, for the sole purpose of carrying, and seeing carried, everything for him and others across the lake; and am sensible that he did agree with Colonel Arnold to do the whole business for the public, as he has crafts and carriages convenient for that purpose, for twenty shillings per day; and I do verily believe the method they now have taken, will, in the main, amount to four or five pounds per day. This Mr. John Spardin, to my knowledge, is a very worthy man, and is both willing and capable to do the business for us, so that we may not be in want of provision as often as we now are; and I believe him to be a hearty son of liberty." ("Jour. of N. Y. Prov. Congress," Vol. II, p. 67.)

† *See* Beardsley's "Reminiscences," p. 16.

‡ The peaceful Quakers, however, had settled at Queensbury, in the following Revolution sympathising with the Crown. Ethan Allen, a ringleader, was priced at £150.

CHAPTER II.

AY TENTH, 1775, Ticonderoga was captured by a party of volunteers, under the command of Benedict Arnold* and Ethan Allen,† with whom was associated Bernard Romans, the able and celebrated engineer. Romans improved the occasion to seize Fort George. It is true that local traditions have assigned this capture to others; yet, when we examine the claim, it is clear that it was instituted by those who knew nothing whatever of the state of the fort at the time. The traditional account says, in substance, that on the reception of the news

---

* Benedict Arnold is, perhaps, one of the most thoroughly abused men of the Revolution. Even Sparks, who tried to treat him fairly, reveals a strong prejudice, and portrays him as practically disgraced when superseded at Ticonderoga; whereas the confidence of the authorities was unimpaired, he being returned afterwards to the lake in a still higher capacity; and when, a little later, Washington devised the overland expedition against Quebec, upon the success of which he believed the salvation of the country depended, he turned at once to Arnold as the man for the work; while, down to the very hour of his treason, Arnold occupied the highest place in his estimation. In connection with his Ticonderoga experience, the following letter to Arnold may well have a place:

" COLLONY OF THE MASSACHUSETTS BAY
" *Watertown* June 1, 1775.

" SIR

"This Congress have Received yours of the 19 and 23d of May ult, a copy of has been sent to N. Hampshire & Capt. Brown & Capt. Phelps they highly approve of and take great satisfaction in the acquisitions you have made at Ticonderoga Crown Point on The Lake &c; as to the State you are in respecting your Provision &c we have advices from Connecticut and New York that ample preparation is making with the Greatest Dispatch in those two collonies from whence you may Depend on being seasonably supplied—they are Sorry to meet with Repeated Requests from you that some Gentleman be sent to succeed you in command; they assure you that they place The Greatest Confidence in your Fidelity Knowledge Courage and Good Conduct and they Desire that you at present Dismiss the Thought of Quitting Your Important Command at Ticonderoga Crown Point Lake Champlain &c and you are hereby requested to continue your command over the forces raised by this colony Posted at those several Places at least untill the Collony of New York or Connecticut shall take on them the maintaining & commanding the same agreeable to an order of the Continental Congress." (MSS. in Mass. Archives.)

† The following unpublished letter, addressed to the Connecticut committee, suggests the origin of the disorder that prevailed immediately after the capture of the post:

"SIR Whereas the Fortress of Ticonderoga has fallen into the Hands of the Colonies together with the Ordnance Stores &c and whereas Capt. William Delaplace has in the fort

of the Battle of Lexington, one Daniel Parks, of Sandy Hill, raised a band of volunteers, and afterwards marched to Fort George, which, together with "Fort Gage," was garrisoned by two companies of artillery. On his arrival at the fort, he drove the garrison down the lake to Diamond Island, where they intrenched. The commander, it appears, was captured, and, on surrendering his sword, is represented as telling Parks that his neck would "stretch" for this "thing."

The story, in former days, edified the villagers of Sandy Hill and vicinity, and, latterly, has crept into print, being embodied in patriot historical sketches and sermons; but it is, nevertheless, destitute of a real foundation, as we have already seen that the fort was without a garrison at the time. The facts in connection with the transfer of Fort George to the American authorities are narrated in the following petition of John Nordberg, now preserved in the "N. Y. Miscellaneous Papers," Vol. XXXI, p. 15:

"THE MOST RESPECTABLE GENTLEMEN,
  "PROVINCIAL CONGRESS IN NEW YORK.

"I beg leave to represent to the most respectable Congress this circumstance.

"I am a native of Sweden, and have been persecuted for that, I have been against the French faction there.

"I have been in His Britanick Magesty's Service sinse January 1758.

"I have been twice shot through my body here last war in America, & I am now 65 years old—reduced of age, wounds & and gravels, which may be seen by Doctor Jones's certificate.

"1773. I got permission in Jamaica to go to London where I petition to be an Invalid officer, but as a foreigner I could not enjoy a commission in England, or Ereland His Magisty was graciously pleased to give me the allowance for Fort George 7 shilling sterling per day, with liberty to live where I please in America, because the fort has been abandoned this 8 year and only 2 men remain there for to assist any express going between New York and Canada. I arrived here in New York last year in September with intention to live in New York: as I heard nothing els than disharmony amongst Gentlemen which was not agreeable to my age. I resolved to go to Fort George and live there in a little Cottage as a Hermit, where I was very happy for 6 months.

"The 12 of May last Mr. Romans* came & took possession of Fort

---

Ninety Gallons of Rum of his own property which is greatly wanted for the Refreshment of the Fatigued Soldiery—This is therefore to desire the Treasurer of the Colony of Connecticut to Pay him the Sd Wm De la Place Eighteen Pounds Eleven Shillings & Nine pence Lawfull money, as the Rum is appropriated for the use of the Garrison—Your Compliance will oblige the Garrison

"and your Humble Servant
"ETHAN ALLEN Commandt of Ticond."
(Conn. Rev. MSS.)

* "Bernard Romans was born in Holland; but, in early life removed to England, where he studied the profession of an engineer, and was employed by the British Government in America

George, Mr. Romans behaved very genteel and civil to me. I told that I did not belong to the army and may be considered as a half pay officer invalid, and convinced him that I was pleagd with Gravell, Mr. Romans give me his passport to go to New Lebanon for to recover my health, & he told me that in regard to my age, I may go where I please.

"As I can't sell any bill for my subsistance, & I can't live upon wind and weather, I therefore beg and implore the most respectable Congress permission to go to England, and I intend to go to my native country, I could have gone away secret so well as some others have done, but I will not upon any account do such a thing — I hope the most respectable will not do partially to refuse me, because major Etherington, Captain Brown, Captain Kelly which is in the army have been permitted to go to England, and it may happen they return here again on actual Service, which old age & infirmities render me incapable of.

"As it is the custom among the Christian nations and the Turks, that they give subsistance to every Prisoner according to their Rank should the most respectable Congress, have any claim upon me to be a prisoner here, I hope they will give me my subsistence from th 12 of May last, according to My Rank as Captain I implore the favor of the most respectable Congress answer. I have the honour to remain with great respect,

"GENTLEMEN
 "Your most obed^t humble Servant
  "JOHN NORDBERG."

"NEW YORK, decemb^r 1775."

It appears that Romans, finding it impossible to manage the leaders at Ticonderoga (*See* "Conn. Hist. Coll.," Vol. 1, p. 169), improved the opportunity to perform a separate service. How he conducted * the

---

sometime before the Revolution. Subsequently he was employed as a botanist by the same government; and, while in New York, engaged in the publication of a natural history of Florida, he was offered a position as military engineer by the New York Committee of Safety. In the capacity, he submitted to Congress, on the 18th of September, 1775, plans for fortifications to be erected in the Highlands, opposite West Point. Colonel Romans remained in service (Captain Pennsylvania Artillery, Feb. 8, 1776) until near the close of the war, when he was captured at sea by the British, *en route* from New Haven or New London to Charleston, S. C. He is reported to have died about 1783." (Boynton's " West Point," p. 21n.)

* The following accounts from unpublished MSS. may be of interest here :

"STILLWATER 6th o $Clock$ P.M 1775

"SIR I have sent three barrels of Pork to Pawlet & one to Fort George with two barrels of Flower that that I Bought of Esqr. Palmer who has sent his son with a waggon to Carry the same—There is due to Esqr. Palmer for the flower & grain for the horses, Four Pounds two shillings, which sum Please to Pay him & take his Rec$t$. for the same, I shall get the Wagon forward as fast as Possible. Esqr. Palmer can inform how we have proceeded. I am Sir yours—

" JNO. STEVENS
" To Capt. B. ROMANS.—"

" Recd. from Barnard Romans Three Pounds Sixteen Shillings L. money of Connett. for Traveling expence— rec$d$. P— JNO. STEVENS—
" May 5. 1775.—"
" Recd. Stonacbice 5th May 1775. of Benj$n$. French two pounds sixteen shillings on acco$r$ of Barnard Romans—rec$d$. P me—
£2. 16 0   " JNO. STEVENS."

affair, is shown by Nordberg's petition; but as he failed to give any public account of the transaction, whatever credit his act may have deserved was appropriated by others for the benefit of Daniel Parks, the inscription upon whose gravestone, however, represents no more than that he was the man who "took the key" at "Lake George."*

The only printed reference to this subject that appeared, beyond what is contained in the American Archives, before the writer gave his attention to the subject, is contained in a letter by Governor Tryon to the Earl of Dartmouth, dated Aug. 7, 1775, in which he alludes to "Captn Nordbergh who was taken prisoner at Lake George the 12th of April last." ("Coll. Doc.," Vol. VIII, p. 597.) The date is too early by one month.

The accounts of Bernard Romans† with the Colony of Connecticut show something of his movements at this time. One item runs "To Expen^s on road at mead^w runbridge & Fort George: 16 men. £1. 10."

That Daniel Parks may have been one of the sixteen men employed in various ways by Mr. Romans, at a cost of "£1. 10," is not unlikely, though this is a mere conjecture, destitute of proof. Nevertheless, the winter-evening gossip of the region made Parks something of a hero, averring that he was commander of the fort after the "capture." A nephew of Parks, some years since, also stated that, "while his Uncle Daniel Parks commanded at Fort George, a party of Tories and Indians

---

"Fort George 16*th* May 1775. Rec*d*. of Bernard Romans Esq*r*. the Sum of £4. 2.—for the use of the Colony of Massachusetts—   PETER CASWELL.—"

"Rec*d*. Stonacbicie 5*th* May 1775—of Mr. Bernard Romans Sixteen Pounds N York Currency in full for 4 bb/*s* of Pork—
£16. 0: 0—£n.—Lm. y.   P. me BENJN. FRENCH."

"Rec*d*. at Bennington this 3*d* May 1735 of Bernard Romans the sum of Sixty Pounds Law full money of Connect*r*. for the use of the Colony.
"ELISHA PHELPS."

"Col. of Conn   To   Josiah Stoddard   D
"To my Expences at Fort George while Comisary of Stores 11 days   £11. 6
"To horse traveling once to Skensboro:, once to Fort George
"300 Miles from Salisbury—p 3*d*."   } 3. 15.--
                                         ("Conn. Rev. Papers," Vol. III, pp. 28-35.)

* The following is the inscription chiselled upon a white marble tablet:

"In memory of
DANIEL PARKS
Who departed this life
March the 3 1818, aged
78, one of the veterans of the
Revolutionary war. he was
the man who took the key
from the brittish officer at
Lake George in 1775."

"The little rural (and family) burying ground containing this grave," says a correspondent, who sends the above, "is in the town of Moreau, Saratoga County, on the south bank of the Hudson (from the Big-Falls to Sandy-Hill, the course of the Hudson is eastward), and about one mile from Baker's Falls, the starting point of the base lines of the great Kayaderosseras Patent."

† Published, in full, from the original MS., by the author, in "Lake George: its Scenes and Characteristics." Appendix I.

killed, at South Glens Falls, his brother Ephraim Parks and their Father Elijah Parks; & captured his other son Elijah Parks, Jun., & carried him to Canada. (Lewis Brown, a brother-in-law of Ephraim Parks having escaped by the way.) This happened during the autumn of 1775. The Tories & Indians were pursued by Ferguson, a refugee from the Great Bend above Glen's Falls, & commanded by one Richardson, who wished to obtained the title deeds which Elijah Parks had received from John Glen. The principal purpose, however, was to *avenge the Capture of Fort George*, for which Daniel Parks had frequently been threatened. He, however, escaped, although laid-in-wait-for by the Richardson party, which (after the Glen's Fall massacre) returned *via* Schroon Lake to Montreal."*

A good-sized volume might be filled with similar narrations, connected with this and kindred subjects of the time; yet, it will be found, by a careful examination, that the accounts have no consistency and little foundation, the truth of the matter being like Gratiano's reasons, which were "as two grains of wheat hid in two bushels of chaff." About all that is clear is the fact that broils were constantly taking place at this period all through the lake region, families and neighborhoods being divided on the great question of the day. The Parks family appear to have suffered in body and estate, but not, however, on account of the services of Daniel Parks in the "capture" of Fort George. It is clear that he was never engaged in the military service at all; while the assertion that his progenitor was an officer in the Royal Army is put to flight by an examination of the British Army Lists, which do not contain the name. We must, therefore, dismiss Daniel Parks from connection with the command of this post, and leave undigested and indigestible tales like these to take care of themselves; while we note what certainly occurred after the dismantled fort was taken possession of by Bernard Romans.

The first thing done after Captain Nordberg was dispossessed on May 12, was to prepare for the removal of the cannon from Ticonderoga. We learn this from the letter of Benedict Arnold to the Massachusetts Committee of Safety, where he says:

"I am, with the assistance of Mr. Bernard Romans, making preparations at Fort George for transporting to Albany those cannon that will be serviceable to our Army at Cambridge." In a postscript, he adds: "Since writing the above Mr. Romans concludes going to Albany, to forward carriages for the cannon, &c, and provisions, which will soon be wanted. I beg leave to observe that he has been of great service here, & I think him a very spirited judicious gentleman, who has the service of the country much at heart, and hope he will meet proper encouragement."† ("Amer. Archives," Ser. IV, Vol. II, p. 585.)

---

* MS. letter of an old citizen of that locality.
† Another account furnished by this enterprising individual, though not immediately con-

May 23d, he says: "I have sent expresses to Fort George & Skenesborough to rally the country." (*Ibid*, p. 694.) This was done with reference to an anticipated attack by the British.

Thus, in accordance with a sound policy, they proceeded to reap the fruits of their venturesome undertaking at Ticonderoga.

That one of the main ideas had in view in the capture of Ticonderoga, was the possession of the cannon and stores for revolutionary purposes, is perfectly clear, notwithstanding the subsequent shuffling of the Continental Congress. Arnold and Romans were therefore right in providing for the safety of the cannon; and yet, in a few days, when their eyes were opened to the possibility of the recapture of Ticonderoga by the British, they began to feel less haste than formerly about removing the war material. The Continental Congress, in session at Philadelphia, had, nevertheless, in the meanwhile, taken action, and ordered the captured property to be removed at once to Fort George. Its action was somewhat curious, and shows that the members still saw hope of a peaceable agreement with the mother country, and were willing to return the cannon on the conclusion of a peace. The Resolution of Congress, passed May 18th, runs as follows:

"*Resolved*, Whereas there is indubitable evidence, that a design is formed by the British ministry, of making a cruel invasion from the province of Quebec, upon these colonies, for the purpose of destroying our lives and our liberties, and some steps have actually been taken to carry the said design into execution; and, whereas, several inhabitants of the northern colonies, residing in the vicinity of Ticonderoga, and immediately exposed to incursions, impelled by a just regard for the defence and preservation of themselves and their countrymen from such imminent dangers and calamities, have taken possession of that post, in

---

nected with our subject, may properly be introduced here. It is from the MSS. in Connecticut State Library ("Revolutionary War," Vol. III, p. 25).

"Accts. of monies advanced by Bernard Romans in Expedition against Ticonderoga as
1775   Per acct. kept Per Wm. Nichols Clerk of the Committee.—
May 1st   Expences at Doctr. Wheelers 34s 11 for a Gun dd Mr Mott   £4. 4. 11
          do,   at Dewey's 1s 4—do. Smiths 1s 2—do. at Stockbridge 9s 8   12. 2
          do   at Pearls 1s 4 Exps. from Hartford to Salisbury 43s   2. 4. 4
          Cash pd. Isaac Peck's Exps. from Pittsfield   2. 8
          Expens. at Jewits 1s 4—Provisions Phelps & Heacocks 15s   16. 4
          for Provisions at Bennington 27s 8—do. & Shoes 23s 6   2. 11. 2
          for Cloth for Knapsack 5s 4—horse shoeing 2s   7. 4
          for keepg. Halsey's horse 4s 6. Halsey & Stevens Exps. at Albany 42s 1   2. 6. 7
          for shoeing horse 2s 5—Cloth for Knapsacks 14s   16. 5
          Paid Edward Mott 35s 3d—do. Nichols 6s 6—do. Bull 9s 4   2. 11. 1
          Sundries of Heman Allen   1. 0. —
          for Cloth for Knapsack 5s 4. Exps. at Jericho 30s   1. 15. 4
                                                                         ─────────
                                                                         £19. 8. 4

"The above is a True Copy of the Accot. as kept Per
                                    "Wm Nichols Clerk Comtee."

which was lodged a quantity of cannon and military stores, that would certainly have been used in the intended invasion of these Colonies: this Congress earnestly recommend it to the committees of the cities and counties of New-York and Albany, immediately to cause the said cannon and stores to be removed from Ticonderoga to the south end of lake George; and, if necessary, to apply to the colonies of New-Hampshire, Massachusetts-Bay, and Connecticut, for such an additional body of forces as will be sufficient to establish a strong post at that place, and effectually to secure said cannon and stores, or so many of them as it may be judged proper to keep there. And that an exact inventory be taken of all such cannon and stores, in order that they may be safely returned, when the restoration of the former harmony between Great-Britain and these colonies, so ardently wished for by the latter, shall render it prudent, and consistent with the over-ruling law of self-preservation." ("Journal of Congress," Vol. I, p. 71.)

Thus feeble and apologetic was the language, of that Congress in whose name Ethan Allen pretends to have demanded the surrender of the fort.

But, as already observed, a feeling of alarm arose, and the various authorities of Massachusetts and New-Hampshire remonstrated. Yet, on May 29, Jonathan Trumbull wrote to his brother: "I am glad to find by our letters from New York, that their Congress do not construe the resolution of the Grand Congress to intend an evacuation of Ticonderoga and Crown Point, but only a removal of such stores, &c, as necessary, to Fort George." ("Amer. Archives," Ser. IV, Vol. II, p. 733.) In the meanwhile, also, on the representations of Arnold, the Congress voted to let such cannon remain at Ticonderoga as might be temporarily needed. But, eventually, the alarm subsided, and the British, instead of becoming the aggressors, as was anticipated, yielded the ground far and near, having no sufficient force with which to meet the Americans.

CHAPTER III.

HERE BEING NOW no immediate prospect of an attempt to recapture Ticonderoga, Arnold wrote to the Continental Congress from Crown Point, as follows, under date of May 29: "I have sent to Lake George one brass twelve pounder, six large brass & iron mortars and howitzers, & am making all possible preparation for transporting all the cannon here, and as many as can be spared at Ticonderoga, to Fort George." ("Amer. Archives," Ser. IV, Vol. II, p. 734.)

Still we find that, on June 10th, Ethan Allen is "much surprised that your Honours should recommend to us to remove the artillery to the South End of Lake George, & there make a stand; the consequence of which must ruin the frontier settlements." He wanted the "northerly part of Lake Champlain as a frontier, instead of the south promontory of Lake George." (*Ibid*, p. 734.)

The Massachusetts Provincial Congress also wrote to the Governor of Connecticut, arguing against making "William Henry," meaning Fort George, the base of military operations, showing that, if Ticonderoga were given up, the whole country would be open to the enemy. (*Ibid*, p. 736.) But New York had interpreted the meaning of the Continental Congress aright, and all these protests were, on the whole, quite needless.

While Ticonderoga was still retained, the common cause benefited from the capture, and soon a portion of the artillery found its way to the camp of Washington, at Cambridge.

To transport the artillery, flat-boats were built. The following appears among the memoranda of Arnold:

" To be built on Lake George , 2 flat-bottomed boats, forty feet long, twelve wide, and four deep, with strong knees, well-timbered, &

of four inch oak plank—these may be built at Spardens,* where there is timber & a saw-mill handy. ** There will be wanted at Fort George ten good teams or four yoke of oxen each." It is added, that Colonel Webb may inform himself about procuring them in the neighborhood.

A letter, written by Barnabas Deane, at Albany, about three weeks after the capture of Fort George, shows the condition of things at the fort and in the neighborhood, and, at the same time, testifies to the superior public spirit of the New Englanders; we hear nothing, however, of Daniel Parks. Deane says:

"There are now about 150 men at Crownpoint, 18 men at Ticonderoga, and 25 men at Fort George; which is not one quarter of what is actually necessary for holding those important posts until the cannon &c. can be removed. Everything is in the utmost decay at Ticonderoga and Crownpoint. It struck me with horror, to see such grand fortifications in ruins. Crownpoint is one heap of rubbish, and the wood-work of Ticonderoga not much better. Fort George is a small stone fort, and secure against small arms, but not bear cannonading.

"You no doubt have had an exact acc^t of the ordnance taken at Crownpoint and Ticonderoga. There are four iron mortars and three brass howitzers sent down to Fort George, which came in the boat that I crossed Lake George in. I met 70 men on their march to Crown-

---

* " Memorial of JOHN SPARDING to New York Congress.

" To the Honourable the President and Members of the Provincial Congress now assembled at New York:

" The Memorial of John Sparding, living at Ticonderoga Landing, the north end of Lake George, June 1, 1775, humbly sheweth:

" That your memorialist has, for upwards of six years past, been at a great expense in providing boats and carriages for the ease and convenience of persons travelling this way with their baggage and effects, over the lake, and carrying, at an easy rate; likewise providing batteaus on Lake Champlain, for the conveniency of gentlemen and others travelling to Canada. The unhappy differences now subsisting between the Colonies and the Mother Country, have put a stop to any business your memorialist was formerly engaged in. Your memorialist has, ever since the tenth day of May, (the day on which the fort at Ticonderoga was taken,) assisted with boats, men, &c., in transporting the troops, with their baggage and provisions, over Lake George and the carrying place, upon no other security than a verbal agreement with Colonel Arnold, for twenty shillings, currency, per day, for a perryaugre capable of crossing the lake with seventy men, besides a quantity of provision, and a batteau for carrying expresses; and when there was not a sufficient loading for the perryaugre, to have the privilege of conveying such private property as might offer, of which your memorialist is at present deprived; your memorialist have likewise carted the greatest part of the baggage and provisions over the carrying place, the whole amount of which, to this day, is near seventeen Pounds. And as the gentlemen appointed here have this day intimated to your memorialist that his teams are not to be any more employed, they having brought teams over the lake for said service; your memorialist, therefore, trusting in the known justice and humanity of the gentlemen in New-York, who scorn to let any individual suffer, which must inevitably be the case of your memorialist, unless your goodnes prevents it, by confirming the agreement made by Colonel Arnold: your memorialist therefore humbly hopes, as he has done his utmost endeavour for the good of the common cause, and is disabled at present from providing for his family, you will take the same into consideration. And your memorialist will ever pray.

" J. SPARDING."

("American Archives," Fourth Series, Vol. II, pp. 873-4.)

point to reinforce that place, and believe there will be 500 men there in ten days' time.

"The people of this county have sent a considerable quantity of provision up, and are now sending off men; but they don't act with that spirit and life that the N. England men have on such occasions. Wherever we find a number of *them* settled down, we find men who are ready and willing to go immediately in defence of their country, which is not the case with people here in general, altho' they seem well disposed in the Common Cause.

"I met the Express with the Resolutions of the Congress to remove all the artillery to the south end of Lake George, which gives the greatest anxiety to the inhabitants back, as it leaves the whole of them exposed to the inroads of the Canadians and Indians if they should take up against us, as Fort George is no barrier against them; but if we hold Ticonderoga, which is the key of the whole communication between Canada and the English settlements, it will effectually secure the whole of our frontiers and keep us masters of the Lake. I am really in hopes the matter will be reconsidered in Congress, and that Ticonderoga may be held, as it is a place of the last importance in this critical juncture. There will be a sufficiency of artillery for the fort at Ticonderoga when we have removed 100 pieces to Fort George. This will be handed you by an Express, who carries the opinion of this city and county to the Congress, on this important affair.

"I expect to leave this place in a day or two for home, as I can be of no further service here at present. I never have had so fatigueing a journey in my life as this has been. The intolerable heat in crossing the Lakes in open boats, and being out all night exposed to the cold fogs that arise from stagnated waters, gave me a violent cold, which bro't on a fever for two or three days, but is now in some degree moderated. I can say nothing new to you from home, as you have likely heard from there since I have." (Correspondence of Silas Deane, 1775. "Conn. Hist. Soc. Coll.," pp. 248–9.)

But, in the meanwhile, who was in command at Fort George? This place, not having been otherwise provided for, was controlled from Ticonderoga. There is no trace whatever of the interference of Ethan Allen, but Benedict Arnold boldly asserted his authority, and made himself felt. Fort George was, at this time, a mere dependency of Ticonderoga. The name of the petty officer in charge at the "Landing" does not appear. Soon, however, Colonel Hinman, of Connecticut, superseded Arnold,[*] when the former sent the Connecticut

---

[*] For a short time after the capture of Ticonderoga, Ethan Allen was able to hold his sway, notwithstanding the fact that, as Arnold tells us, in one place, they had, before the capture, agreed "to issue further orders jointly," and, in another, that they had agreed upon a "joint command of the troops." (Letters of May 11 and 29, 1775, in "Archives.") But Allen was soon wearied out by the pertinacity of his rival, who was left to sign himself as the "Commander," without let or hinderance, until superseded by Colonel Hinman. July 31, Schuyler

engineer to examine Fort George. Hinman writes from Ticonderoga, July 3, to the New York Provincial Congress, that Col. Mott had surveyed Fort George, and found it indefensible against artillery. He was of the opinion that "a sufficient number of troops should be stationed at Fort George, with a constant scouting party, in order to prevent any sudden attack of the enemy, & to keep up a safe communication with Albany." ("Cor. N. Y. Prov. Congress," Vol. II, p. 28.) He was also desirous of having a force repair the roads and bridges between Half Moon and Fort George.

In this month, we come to something more tangible. On the 24th of July, Col. Van Schaick made a return of his men, and testified that five companies were there "on actual service at Lake George & the posts adjacent." (*Ibid*, p. 68.) Van Schaick himself was at Albany, one of his captains being at Fort George.

During the summer of 1775, the northern military operations were conducted chiefly within the enemy's lines, and the work of the garrison was confined to the forwarding of reinforcements* and supplies. There was an abundance of hard work, in which they were cheered by the news from the North, where at one time the Americans were likely to meet with permanent success. There were, indeed, rumors of flank movements on the part of the British, while a lawless band from Vermont, June 5th, improved the disturbed condition of public affairs to descend from the region of the Green Mountains to break up the court sitting at Fort Edward, with the intention of "abolishing the law." But, fortunately, Captain Mott was at that time marching from Connecticut with reinforcements for Ticonderoga, and, being notified of the intentions of these roving ruffians, who were mostly " poor debtors," with nothing to lose by a reign of anarchy, he marched to the relief of the court, and drove the desperadoes back to their native fastnesses among the hills, where men of their stamp had long been accustomed to

---

writes, from Ticonderoga, that "a controversy has arisen between Allen & Warner; the former, you will perceive is left out altogether by the Green-Mountain Boys." ("Cor. N. York Prov. Congress," p. 43.)

* "Order to Mr. DALLY, (1775)

"You are Desired By the General Committee of the Association for the City & County of New York To Proceed With all Convenient Speed with the Carpenters here named

Daniel Lawrence	Barnet Christopher
James Sharp	Isaac Dodge
Thomas Hunt	Jno. German

To Albany and there Apply to the Committee for what Assistance you may want In Forwarding you to Lake George Where you are to build scows and what other Crafts may there Be Wanting and when you have Completed all that is to be Built or Repared there, you are to return directly to New York and you are to have the Following Stipulated Wages from the Day you Sett of To the Day you Return to New York Except you are detained By your own Neglect By the Way John Daly foreman 12s per Day and found Every Thing Except Liquor—all the rest of the above Named Carpenters to have nine Shilling & Sixpence per Day & Everything found Except Liquor." ("N. Y. Misc. Papers," pp. 34, 93.)

scenes of lawlessness and disorder. With this effort, the operations of these lawless men, so far as this region was concerned, but elsewhere, led on by designing men, they created great dissensions.* *See* (" Corr. Prov. Congress," Vol. II.)

Finally, the summer wore away, and winter settled down up the lake, covering St. Sacrament with a bridge of ice hardly adapted to advance the military operations.

But when the season of activity opened again, the scene on the lake became more animated than before, and the slow-moving barge was, in a measure, superseded by the light batteaux, which everywhere ploughed the lake, impelled by hurrying oars. Accordingly, Fort George assumed all of its earlier importance, and became a locality of deep interest to both soldier and civilian.

But, to make the situation clear, it must be stated, in brief, that during the previous year, 1775, the campaign in Canada had been conducted by Generals Schuyler and Montgomery, the army, as we have seen, being supplied by transports on Lake George. Early in that year, Schuyler had been forced from the field by disease, leaving his coadjutor to capture Fort St. John and Montreal. At Quebec the brave Montgomery fell in the assault, and his defeated troops wintered at Sillery; in the spring, receiving General Wooster as their commander.

But the second attempt upon Quebec also failed, and, for the lack of reinforcements, the Americans were under the necessity of retreating from Canada. The command of this army was now given to General Thomas, and was included in the department commanded by Schuyler. General Thomas, though an efficient officer, strove in vain to stay the tide of defeat. April 17, 1776, he left Fort George, and, the next day, five hundred troops followed him down the lake; while, two days later, it was estimated that fifteen hundred were already on the way, and expecting to make a "respectable figure before Quebec." But they all failed to realize their wishes, while General Thomas died of the smallpox, which erelong decimated the army, and inspired deep dismay.

At this period, some distinguished visitors reached Fort George. These were Benjamin Franklin and his associates, Chase and Carroll, who had been appointed by Congress, as commissioners, to visit and treat with the Canadian authorities. They were also accompanied by the brother of Commissioner Carroll, a clergyman who afterwards became the Roman Catholic Bishop of Baltimore.

The party ascended the Hudson by sloop and batteau, and crossed

---

* The leaders in Vermont who had previously encouraged and led the way in the disturbances of the times, discountenanced this act; but some of them relapsed into their old ways. Among these was Ethan Allen, the leader of the "Bennington mob" of 1774. May 25, 1779, he fell upon the peaceable inhabitants of Brattleboro', calling out the appeal of Samuel Minott to Gov. Clinton, wherein, he says, "Our situation is truly critical and distressing, we therefore most humbly beseech your Excellency to take the most speedy & effectual Measures for our Relief; otherwise our Persons and Property must be at the disposal of Ethan Allin, which is more to be dreaded than death with all its terrors." ("N. Y. Doc. Hist.," Vol. IV, p, 581.)

from the Falls of the Hudson to the lake by land. Though charged with a grave mission, all were fully alive to the romantic interest of the region through which they had passed; but they arrived at Lake St. Sacrament too early in the season to enjoy its rare scenery. The ice on the lake had just broken up, and the hills were verdureless and gray. Speaking of the approach to the lake, Carroll says, in the journal:

"*18th.* We set off for Wing's tavern about twelve o'clock this day, and reached Fort George about two o'clock; the distance is about eight miles and a half;—you cannot discover the lake until you come to the heights surrounding it,—the descent from which to the lake is nearly a mile;—from these heights you have a beautiful view of the lake for fifteen miles down it. Its greatest breadth during these fifteen miles does not exceed a mile and a quarter, to judge by the eye, which, however, is a very fallacious way of estimating distances. Several rocky islands appear in the lake, covered with a species of cedar here called hemlock." (Carroll's "Journal," p. 49.)

The philosopher, Franklin,* and his party embarked in a flat-bottomed boat, thirty-six feet long, propelled in part by "a square sail or blanket," and proceeded down the lake. Before starting, however, they took a general view of the situation, and examined Fort George, concerning which, Mr. Charles Carroll wrote in the journal, as follows:

"Fort George is in as ruinous a condition as Fort Edward, it is a small bastion, faced with stone, and built on an eminence commanding the head of the lake.—There are some barracks in it, in which the troops were quartered, or rather *one* barrack, which occupied almost the whole space between the walls. At a little distance from this fort," the writer adds, "and to the westward of it, is the spot where Baron Dieskau was defeated by Sir William Johnson. About a quarter of a mile to the westward the small remains of Fort William Henry are to be seen across a little rivulet which forms a swamp." (*Ibid*, p. 49.)

May 21st, General Schuyler had established his head-quarters at Fort George, where he was visited by Mr. Graydon, who came to bring money for the troops. Speaking of the road from Fort Edward to Fort George, Graydon says:

"It was almost an entire wood, acquiring a deeper gloom, as well as from the general prevalence of pines, as from its dark extended covert, being presented to the imagination as an appropriate scene for the treasons, stratagems and spoils of savage hostility."† ("Memoirs," p.

---

* General Schuyler says, at this time, in one of his letters: "A vile ague seized me some days ago, but Doctor *Franklin* and the other gentlemen administered such a number of doses of *Peruvian* bark, that it has left me, and I hope that I shall last at least this campaign." ("Am. Archives," Ser. iv, Vol. v, p. 1098.)

† While on these subjects, we may also call attention to "Blind Rock," a place where the Indians are said to have tortured their prisoners, put out their eyes, and indulged in other characteristic pastimes. The locality is pointed out in a letter addressed to the author, by the Rev. A. S. Fennel, of Glen's Falls. He writes:

"'Blind Rock,' one of the boulders which are numerous in this region, lies about half way

142.) Again, speaking of Bloody Pond, near Fort George, on the occasion of his approach, he says: "The descending sun had shed a browner horror on the wilderness; and as we passed the Dismal pool, we experienced that transient emotion of commisseration which is natural to the mind when contemplating past events involving the fall of friends, the fortunes of war, and the sad condition of human kind." (*Ibid.*)

General Schuyler, at this time, occupied such narrow quarters that he appears to have had few facilities for extending hospitalities, yet he had his family with him, and kept his table furnished with wine. He did not invite every one to drink it, however; and Graydon, who was in sympathy with Schuyler and hostile to "Yankees," speaks, with satisfaction, of the contemptuous and undignified manner in which Schuyler, in moments of forgetfulness, allowed himself to treat certain of the New England officers under his command. This unfortunate peculiarity, undoubtedly, led the way to the loss of his place, and deprived the country of the services of an otherwise valuable officer and an upright man.

At this time Schuyler had an abundance of batteaux, and could move three regiments at a time. Accordingly, he was very busy forwarding troops. He had, also, a flat-bottomed boat with sails. It was capable of carrying two hundred barrels, and made the trip in five days. Eleven batteaux carried thirty barrels each, and, with seven men, made the trip in four days.

On the 26th of May, he had only one hundred and eighteen men at the post, while but forty-five were fit for duty, and these, even, were "raw & undisciplined." He well remarks, that a force so trifling "leaves us exposed to the insults of any very inconsiderable party, who may destroy our boats & buildings." ("Archives," Ser. IV, Vol. VI, p. 582.)

June 15, Schuyler says: "As to fortifying Ticonderoga & Fort George, and opening the road by Wood Creek, it is utterly impossible with the men I now have left; they are so fully employed in batteaus &c., that I do not believe there is now a relief at Fort George for a subaltern's guard." (*Ibid*, p. 912.)

In June, General Gates succeeded General Thomas in the command at the North, but his army having been driven from Canada within the department of Schuyler, he was, therefore, properly subordinate to him, as a vote of Congress finally decided on June 12th; yet, on the 17th, Gates issued the following from his head-quarters at Ticonderoga:

---

up the first hill we reach in passing to Lake George—about 2½ miles from this village, & 20 rods East of the plank-road. It was upon the margin of the old high-way, which, at that place, was on the same spot as the old military road. It is a little more than half way from Fort Edward to the Lake, & is on high & dry ground, while for considerable distance on this side the ground must have been originally somewhat wet & swampy. This rock is repeatedly mentioned by name in our early town records, as a land-mark recognized & well known. The legends in regard to this as a place of Indian resort, & where their captives suffered, are too numerous for me to attempt to indicate."

"SIR: I understand that there is a wanton waste of powder at your post, in firing a morning & evening gun, and in unnecessary salutes. It is my positive order that this practice be immediately discontinued, and no ammunition expended on any account whatever, except in opposition to the attacks of the enemy. I am, sir, your humble servant.

"HORATIO GATES, Major-General.
"To the Commanding officer at Fort George."

July 17, Gates also wrote from Ticonderoga to Colonel Gansevoort, in command at the fort, to prevent desertions, as "some villains may perhaps feign themselves sick" to the end of escaping the service. He also complains that letters are broken open and detained at Fort George.

John Trumbull wrote to Colonel Read, from head-quarters, July 22, 1776:

"SIR: By the General's order, I wrote you four or five days since, desiring you to collect all the well at Fort George of every corps and return to the army with them. Perhaps you have not received that letter. There is now a still more urgent necessity for your immediate return, as you are appointed to the command of a brigade, with whom your presence is absolutely necessary. You will therefore, sir, on receipt of this, immediately collect all who are able to return to duty, and repair with them to this place as soon as possible.

"I am, sir, your very humble servant
"JOHN TRUMBULL.
"To Colonel READ."

("Amer. Archives," Vol. I, p. 511.)

The following distinctly indicates who was the actual commander at Fort George:

"FORT GEORGE, 30th July, 1776

"SIR: I have only time to acknowledge the receipt of your favor of the 13th Instant which came to my hand this morning And in answer thereto inform you that the Companies of Col. Wyncoops Regiment which were here are gone to Ticonderoga and some to Skenesborough.

"I am Sir your Hum¹ Svt
"PETER GANSEVOORT Lt. Colonel
"Commanding Fort George.
"To JOHN McKESSON."

(*Ibid*, p. 93

CHAPTER IV

T THIS PERIOD, the army under Gates was suffering from infectious diseases, and especially from the small-pox, which led to the establishment of a general hospital at Fort George. On this subject, Schuyler* wrote to Washington, July 12th, as follows:

"By advice of the General Officers, I have ordered all the sick to Fort George. Two houses, capable of containing about three hundred and fifty, are ready for their reception, and a sufficient quantity of boards is collected, under which to shelter the remainder comfortably until hospitals can be erected." (Force's "Archives," Ser. v, Vol. I, p. 232.)

In a letter, of the same date, to Governor Trumbull, he says: "I believe the last of these unhappy people will be there this evening, or to-morrow at farthest." (*Ibid*, p. 237.)

The terrible condition of the army, at this time, is shown by General Gates, writing from Ticonderoga to Washington. July 29th, he says:

"Everything about this army is infected with pestilence: the clothes, the blankets, the air, and the ground they walk upon. To put this evil from us, a General Hospital is established at Fort George, where there are now between two & three thousand sick, and where every infected person is immediately sent." (*Ibid.*)

July 31, Trumbull writes to Colonel Ganesvoort:

"It has been told the General that some officers at your post (not yourself) have presumed to give furloughs to the sick, when discharged from the hospital. You will inquire into this, and let any gentleman who may have done it heretofore know, that if he is found guilty of

---

* Schuyler wrote to Governor Trumbull, July 25: "Before I last went to Crown Point, I gave directions to Lieutenant-Colonel Buell to collect all the boards he possibly could for erecting hospitals for the sick at Fort George, & temporary barracks for the troops wherever they might be."

conduct so unprecedented and so prejudicial to the service, he will be immediately put in arrest, and tried for his presumption and breach of orders by a general court-martial." (*Ibid*, p. 698.)

About this time Baron Woedtke died at Fort George, though the exact date of the event cannot now, at least by the writer, be ascertained.* General Wilkinson also tells us, in his "Memoirs," of his own narrow escape at this place:

"Disappointment & chagrin exasperated my desease, until it was considered necessary to remove me to the south end of Lake George, under the personal attendance of Doctor Jonathan Potts, the surgeon-general. There aid, in spite of medical, I was reduced to the last extremity; every hope of my recovery had expired; I was consigned to the grave, and a coffin was prepared for my accommodation." ("Memoirs," Vol. 1, p. 86.)

---

* The following documents bear on the subject of Baron Woedtke's death:

"FORT GEORGE, *July* 20, 1776.

"SIR: I have to inform you that I still lie in a very weak and low situation. I find the Canadians are gone on to Albany. I beg leave to advise the General to recall them to this place, with the person who has assumed to himself the title of Major, one Mr. Hare, who, when he arrives here, I pray may be put under arrest, and deprived of that Commission which he has assumed to himself, which, I assure you, I never authorised him to take.

"I have the honor to be your Excellency's most obedient Servant,

"BARON DE WOEDTKE.

"To Major-General GATES."

("Amer. Archives," Ser. v, Vol. 1, p. 475.)

Gates to President of Congress, Ticonderoga, July 29, 1776.

"Brigadier Baron de Woedtke went by my permission, to the General Hospital, at Lake George, about a fortnight ago. His health was indeed so much impaired, that I doubt his recovery." (*Ibid*, p. 649.)

General Gates write to Congress, from Ticonderoga, August 6, 1776, as follows:

"Brigadier-General Baron de Woedtke died at Lake George the beginning of last week. He was buried with the honors due to his rank." (*Ibid*, p. 796.)

"Baron de Woedtke had been for many years an officer in the army of the King of Prussia, and had risen to the rank of Major. Coming to Philadelphia with strong letters of recommendation to Dr. Franklin from persons of eminence in Paris, he was appointed by Congress a brigadier-general on the 16th of March and ordered to Canada. He died at Lake George, and was buried with the honors due to his rank." ("Washington's Writings," Vol. IV, p. 6.)

General Gates also wrote to Doctor Potts, as follows:

"TICONDEROGA *August* 12, 1776.

"SIR: I am informed that Baron de Woedtke, some time before his death, made a solemn declaration to you of matter that highly concerns the interest of the United States. You will please forthwith communicate to me the substance of the Baron's declaration. The bearer, Mr. Lucas, has my orders to wait for your letter, and return with it immediately to me.

"I would not wish to give unnecessary trouble; once a fortnight is full often enough to make general return of the Hospital.

"I desire Dr. Stringer may come here as soon as he arrives at Fort George, and bring with him a Surgeon, properly provided for, for the Service of the fleet.

"I am &c   HORATIO GATES.

"To Dr. POTTS at Fort George."

("Amer. Archives," Ser. v, Vol. 1, p. 924.)

The Baron used to say, very often: "Ah Liberdy is a fine ding, I like Liberdy: Der Koernig von Prusse is a great man for Liberdy." (*Ibid*, p. 139.)

Wilkinson revived, nevertheless, and lived to play an important part in connection with subsequent events.

A letter from Ticonderoga, of August 5th, 1776, says that "the sick, about one thousand five hundred, are at Fort George, and recruiting fast." ("Amer. Archives," Ser. v, Vol. 1, p. 857.)

The following official reports from Dr. Potts to General Gates throw much light upon the subject under consideration:

"FORT GEORGE, *August* 8. 1776.

"HONOURED SIR: The return of the sick remaining in the General Hospital, which you were pleased to order to be made weekly, will be delivered to you by Captain Craig. I hope you will not attribute its late appearance at this time to any neglect on my part, as I can with truth assure your Honour nothing is left undone in my power to reduce every matter relative to the hospital into order. The number of the sick being great, they employ our whole time; and having but one clerk, who has to enter the names of every person admitted, discharged, died, or deserted, as well as to superintend the issuing of provisions, makes it almost impossible to comply with your orders so punctually as I would wish.

"I am your Honour's obedient and very humble servant
"JONA. POTTS."

"FORT GEORGE *Aug^t* 24th. 1776.

"HONOURED SIR: Your Honour's favour of the 23^d instant by Mr. Watson, I received this morning. I assure your Honour I have spared him from our Huckster's Shop every article in my power. What keeps Mr Henry with the Medicines I am at loss to know, I sent one of my Mates three days since to Albany to expedite his coming, and to purchase if possible some Articles we are wholly out of. I have also wrote to the Committee of Albany & Salisbury to send me as soon as possible all the old Linen Rags they can procure, as well as to recommend to the farmers & others to cure a quantity of Herbs for the use of the Hospital, it pains me much to think of our destitute situation, for should your Honour be attacked we have have not bandages or lint to dress fifty

---

Again, Trumbull writes to Lieutenant-Colonel Gansevoort from Ticonderoga, July 31, 1776:

"SIR: The bearer, Major Hubly, late Major of Brigade to General Woedtke, comes to take an inventory and appraisement of the late Baron Woedtke's goods. This you will permit him to do, and to bring such goods &c., as he shall think proper, with the will, to this place, where Colonel D'Haas proposes to administer on the Estate."

The Baron stands poorly in Wilkinson's "Memoirs." Speaking of his meeting with the Baron in Philadelphia, a Roman Catholic prelate says:

"Though I had frequently seen him before, yet he was so disguised in furs, that I scarce knew him, & never beheld a more laughable object in my life. Like other Prussian officers, he appears to me as a man who knows little of polite life, and yet has picked up so much of it in his passage through France, as to make a most awkward appearance." ("Life Arch. Bishop Carroll," p. 42.)

Somewhere near Fort George, the remains of the poor Baron lie in their unknown grave.

men, I can with confidence assure your Honour nothing shall be left undone in my power to procure every necessary for the good of the Army in my Line of Duty—I heartily thank your Honour for your Orders respecting the Returns of the Regimental Surgeons,* as well as your approving my sentiments in regard to D^r Mc Crea—I was greatly surprised in having some patients sent here with the small-pox from the new levies. I have strictly examined them & cannot find that they have been inoculated, should I discover such a thing, shall be careful to transmit to your Honour every matter relative to it—as well as effectually secure the patients.—One thing I would recommend to your Honour's Notice, which I hope you will not think foreign to my Duty, as the Army is greatly exposed to Intermittents & bilious complaints from their situation I am humbly of opinion it would conduce to their Health if every Man was allowed half a Gill of Bitter Rum p^r day, it can be made with four pounds of Gentian Root & two pounds of Orange peel to a Hogshead if these articles are not to be had, the Regimental Surgeons

* Return of the sick of the General Hospital at Fort George, from the 12th to the 26th July, 1776, inclusive:

REGIMENTS.	ADMITTED.	DISCHARGED.	DIED.	DESERTED.	REMAINING.
Colonel Patterson's,	73	26	8	...	39
Colonel Burrells',	164	69	8	2	85
Colonel Bond's,	116	31	3	...	82
Artillery,	56	24	...	...	32
Colonel De Haas's,	118	22	...	...	95
Colonel Bedel's,	21	1	...	...	20
Colonel Reed's,	127	40	3	...	84
Colonel Maxwell's,	172	83	5	...	84
Colonel Porter's,	59	9	3	...	47
Colonel Greaton's,	43	15	...	...	28
Colonel Wind's,	129	35	5	...	89
Colonel Stark's,	105	6	3	...	96
Batteau men,	2	...	...	...	2
Artificers,	12	...	...	...	12
Colonel Van Schaick's,	113	55	5	...	53
Colonel Wynkoop's,	14	3	...	...	11
Colonel Wayne's,	6	4	...	...	2
Colonel Van Dykes,	4	1	...	...	3
Colonel St. Clair's,	83	13	0	...	64
Colonel Irvine's,	31	2	1	1	27
Colonel Poor's,	49	...	...	...	49
	1497	439	51	3	1004
men for Nurses,					106
Total,					1110

("Archives," Ser. v, Vol. I, p. 854.

can readily procure some Snake root, Centaury or Dogwood Bark, which will answer as nearly as well—Inclosed have sent your Honour the returns of the Hospital, on which I have only to observe, that we have a greater Number than appears from the return, owing to the names being struck out from the Hospital Book but I still detain them under the name of convalescents, who will be sent forward in a day or two. I have taken the Liberty to send your Honour a tolerably good weather & a Cask with some Beans, squashes, Cucumbers & a few small Melons, the moment I can procure any good vinegar it shall be forwarded to you.

"I am your Honours most Obedient & very humble Servant
"Jonⁿ. Potts."
(Gates' MSS. in N. Y. Hist. Society, p. 178.)

About this time, there came to be a feeling of general alarm, and Gates wrote to Schuyler, Sept. 6th, that he would be obliged if he would "immediately reinforce For: George with all the troops that be spared from Albany." As there were too few men to forward provisions over the lake, he would send Colonel Phinney's New Hampshire Regiment to the fort "to batteau the flour thence."

Sept. 18, Major Carnes wrote to Gates, from Fort George, "the sickness here rather abates." There was, also, an insufficiency of men.

Oct. 1, Schuyler wrote to Gates on the strength of information sent him by General Washington:

"It is probable that a blow is meditated on the communication. The Garrison at Fort George* is too weak to encounter a vigorous attack, and as the fate of the army depends on the regularity of the supplies, you will please detach a battalion to its support, which may again join you in time, should General Arnold be unable to keep the Lake. A sufficiency of batteaus should for that purpose be kept at Fort George." ("Amer. Archives," Ser. v, Vol. ii, p. 833.)

Oct. 11, Dayton's regiment was ordered to Fort George with despatch.

Oct. 15th, the New York Committee of Safety requested liberty of the Continental Congress "to send a Commissary to Ticonderoga and Fort George, in order to take Charge" of the hides wasted at those posts. (*Ibid*, p. 250.)

---

* " Meeting of the Committee with General Schuyler & Lieut Col Gansevoort Saraytoga
"22d. October 1776
" 1st. Marked the Officers fit for service.
" 2nd. Agreed to appoint Col Van Shaick's Regiment to recruit:

" Capt Andrew Fink   ⎫
" Lieut Charles Parsons ⎬ at Fort George"
" Ensign John Deuny   ⎭

(" New York Miss. Papers.")

The following shows how certain Tories had busied themselves with a futile scheme for the seizure of Fort George. It is the "Information of Stephen Ketchem," under date of October 29th:

"The Information of Stephen Ketchem, who saith

"that on Friday last he saw one Simen Warner, and after Common Compliments Said to this Informer I suppose I may say anything. upon which this Informer Replyed you may. then said Warner, last night I saw Barret Dyre in New Britton, and said Warner Said, it was orders from an Officer above for the tories to form Themselves into a Body. for they expected when our Ermy got Defeated at the northward, the wigs would destroy all the tories they could find, and that the tories where to imbody for Defence. this informer further says he was with the said Warner yesterday and told the Said Warner he came on purpose to see him, and wanted to know if there was any way to escape to the Kings Army to which the said Warner Replyed there was no other to Escape but to go over the North river and so round to our Ermy. this informer asked the said Warner if Barret lived some time in New Britton, and sometimes north of that place with Pallmatire. The said Warner told this Informer that they (the tories) had but a few guns now, but that Dyer told him they expected some up the North river. this Informer asked the said Warner, if he could go to Dyer, he said he thought not for he changed his headquarters often. the said Warner told this Informer that Pallmatier was with Dyre the day before he saw Dyre. this Informer asked Warner how Dyre and the rest of the tories lived. he said about and amongst the rest of their friends. this Informer says Warner further told him that Dyre kept in the woods there till Day light, then came a Cross the Mountains, and by Captain Baldwins and to me good fellows (who is a Corporal in the Grenadier Company) and when he the said Dyre got to good fellows he whistled and good fellows came to him. the said Warner told this Informer that John Savage had with him about five hundred men, and that they had disarmed our Coll^o of the Militia, and taken some guns and other warlike store from him. the said Warner told this Informer that there had been a Post Ridder kept from Army to Army Viz the Kings Armies but lately had been broke up. the Said Warner told this Informer that there was no orders. Particularly now for the tories from Kings Army. But as soon as our headquarters were smash^d the tories would then have orders what to do. this Informer asked the said Warner what they would do as to guns. we the tories will have them all in the district. for he look^d up it there was tories enough in this Government to manage what wigs there were in the same. the Said Warner told this Informer the tories had orders to March in this Alarm to the northward in the name of Congress men and to draw Provisions until they got to Fort George, and then take possession of the same and keep it. the said Warner further said that there would be tories enough going to the Kings Army, If the Militia came back, for that would be their Orders. If any torie was going to be Carryed off only let him Know of It, and there should not a man be carried off, for they would be resqued. and further this Informer saith that Warner told this Informer, If he would come on the hill and Wisstull he would show the Informer People that knew better where Dyre was than he did. the said Warner told this Informer that John Briggs & —— wait that lived with Brigs, was good friends, and that Joseph Chapman could go throu the woods, meaning as this Informer supposes to the Kings Army.

"Signed STEPHEN KETCHEM."
(" New York Mil. Corr.," 25 : 349.)

Oct. 30th, Schuyler says: "the movements of the tories in this quarter give me great reason to suppose that the enemy intended to penetrate by the Mohawk river, or to throw themselves on some part of the communication between this and Fort George." (" Archives," Ser. v. Vol. 1, p. 582.)

Nov. 1st, General Schuyler wrote to the New York Convention that, in case the army went into winter quarters, a garrison of four hundred would be left at Fort George.

General Schuyler also wrote, from Saratoga, to President of Continental Congress: "I hope by Sunday next to have two thousand barrels of flour at the north end of Lake George and Ticonderoga," and that "Colonel Stark's and Colonel Poor's regiments, with that lately belonging to Brigadier Reed (the three amount to about five hundred men) came across Lake George. Two of the regiments I have left at Fort George to forward on the provisions."

Nov. 2d, Schuyler, at Albany, requested Gates to "hasten the regiment to Fort George," as he was afraid that Carlton was seeking to dislodge the Americans from Ticonderoga. But, on the 9th of this month, Gates wrote to Colonel Gansevoort, at Fort George, that "there was not an enemy within a hundred miles of the post." The proposed attack was every way made light of.

Gersham Mott, at Johnstown, writing the 5th of this month to Colonel Lamb, at West Point, says: "Our accounts from Tie are, that Carlton's army are within five miles, and expect them to attack Every Day." (Lamb's MSS.) Yet the attack did not take place.

Nov. 11th, Schuyler wrote to Washington that he had not over four hundred men at Fort George.

Thus, with but a handful of men at this post, winter again came on, while the enlistments expired Dec. 31st, and he was obliged to say that he feared that they could not be prevailed upon to remain after that date. Still the patriots persevered, and Colonel Van Schaick used his best efforts to reorganize his command. The following, addressed to Robert Yates, shows what he accomplished:

"ALBANY *January* 8*th* 1777.

"GENTLEMEN: In my last to the Committee I sent a list of Officers in the first Battalion who had declined the service. I also Recommend Lieu[t] Nathaniel Henry and have by the General's approbation appointed him Lieu[t] advanc'd him money. he has already inlisted near his Complement of men and is with them gone on Service to Fort George, so that the Committee I hope will not fail of appointing him.

"I have also recommended Guy Young & Henry Defendorf for Lieu[ts]; for Ensigns Jonathan Brown, Thomas Hicks, Jacob Ja. Klock, James Bennett, ———— Pecke Recommended by Col. Van Dyck: Ensigns Brown & Hicks have been on the Recruiting Service these four Weeks I wish to receive the approbation of the Committee Soon. A Surgeon ought to be appointed without the least loss of time & sent to me that I may forward him to Fort George, where part of the Regiment is Stationed. I am with perfect Esteem.
     "Your & the Committee's Most H[ble] Serv[t]
       "Goose Van Schaick."
     ("N. Y. Miss. Papers," 38: 443.)

Feb. 2, Colonel Van Schaick writes again:

"At Fort George there is a detachment of nearly two hundred men of mine; many of them are daily falling sick, who with the help of the medicines at that post, and a Surgeon's care, might be enabled in a short time to perform their duties."

Of one, Captain Cobb, he says, that he ordered him "on immediate service with the men under his command, to Fort George, where he has continued ever since with a considerable part of his company." He is pronounced a very faithful and efficient officer. ("Cor. N. Y. Prov. Congress," p. 374.)

CHAPTER V.

INTER FINALLY WORE AWAY, and spring returned, finding the garrison at Fort George unmolested. In the meanwhile, motives of prudence dictated the re-establishment of the hospital at Fort George; and, under date of April 3d, 1777, Dr. Potts writes to General Gates: "I arrived in this city the day before General Schuyler left on his way to Philad: He has ordered to establish the General Hospital at Fort George instead of Mount Independence."

At a later day, the following was addressed to Gates, the writer having in view the enforcement of stricter discipline:

"Fort George *May* 4*th* 1777.

"Honble Sir

"I beg leave to inform your Honour, that there are several Men of Col. Van Schaicks Regiment confined for Crimes not triable by a Regimental Court Martial, one for Desertion and the other for attempting to desert themselves and advising and persuading others to do the like, and as Examples are necessary to be made in the Presence of the Corps the Criminals belong to—I request your Honour to order a Court for their Trial—if you should judge it improper to order the Court to sit at this place, I should be glad to have your Honours Orders what to do with the Criminals—

"I have forwarded the cannon and —— Artillery Stores to Ticonderoga, and am now busy to transport the Provisions a cross—

"I have the Honour to be with
"Great Esteem
"Your very Hble Servt
"C. V. Dyck.

"Honble Maj^r Genl Gates."   (Gates' MSS., p. 70,)

The spring passed in turmoil, and midsummer brought the invasion of Burgoyne. General Patterson, writing to General Gates, from Ticonderoga, May 5, 1777, says:

"By a Scout which this Day Returned I have Certain advice of a party of Indians &c. Who have come up the Lake as far as Crown point, And by their Tracts Taken there Rout towards Lake George—In Consequence of which Captain Whitcomb with one hundred men has gone in pursuit of them, upon whose Return I hope to have the satisfaction of Giving You a good Account of." (Gates' MSS., p. 105.)

The next document is from Gen. Wilkinson, and refers to the commander at Fort George:

FORT GEORGE, *May* 11*th* 1777.

"DEAR & HONOR^D SIR

"I arrived here last Evening and am obliged to wait this Day for the returns of this Garrison. I set out for Tyconderoga Tomorrow Morning with Major Hull's detachment which will be here this evening.

"It is with pleasure I retract my apprehension respecting a detention of Stores at F. Edward, I find the A. Q^r M: at that Post to be one of the few who make the Public Interest a first object, and therefore exerts Himself for His Country; The Capt McCrackin who Commands here wou^d figure better on a Scout than as a Commanding Officer; instead of cooperating with, He Counteracts the Measures of, the Q. M: & Com^{sy}, however as his Conduct is the result rather of Ignorance than design and as He is a brave Man who may be Serviceable in His way, they only wish to have Him removed, as the Command would then devolve on an active and judicious officer.

"T'was Ill natured, Ill judged and impolitic to remove Genl Wayne from Tyconderoga. All the accounts which I now meet from that Post are blacken^d by despair the Child of Terror. Imaginations big with apprehension may easily form an Indian in a Stump, Picture a floating Chunk for a Batteaux full of men. I hope my efforts may be of some Service as they shall not be spared—Inclosed you have the Commissary & Commanding officers returns at F^t Edward, as also the ordinance Stores & A Q^r Masters at this Place The Garrison and Commissary returns I shall enclose you Tomorrow. And am

"My Dear Genl
"Your most obliged
"Obd^t & ready Servt
"JAMES WILKINSON.

"The Commissary has this Minute produced His return, as also the strength of the Garrison both which you have inclosed

"J. W."
(Gates' MSS.)

June 28, Schuyler wrote to Washington, from Albany, that should "General Burgoyne make a push to gain the south part of the Lake, I know of no obstacle to prevent him: comparatively speaking, I have not a man to oppose him; the whole number at the different posts &

on this side of the lake, including Fort George & Skeensborough, not exceeding seven hundred men." (*Ibid*, p. 462.)

June 26, St. Clair writes to Schuyler, that a very large party was reported on the west side of the lake "to fall upon Fort George." They were said to consist of a thousand Indians and Canadians. (*Ibid*, p. 465.)

We have nothing more to present, in connection with the fort, until we reach the period of Burgoyne's actual approach. We find that, as he advanced over Lake Champlain, the alarm increased. Hence the following, written at Fort Edward, by General Schuyler to Washington:

"I am here at the head of a handful of men, not above fifteen hundred, without provision, with little ammunition, not above five rounds to a man, having neither balls, nor lead to make any; the country in the deepest consternation; no carriages to remove the stores from Fort George, which I expect every moment to learn is attacked." ("Washington's Writings," Vol. IV, p. 492.)

According to their anticipations, the Americans were forced to retreat, first from Ticonderoga, and then from Fort George. Dr. Potts reached Albany, and from thence addressed General Gates, as follows:

"My Dear General,

"Your very affectionate letter by John Keys came fortunately safe to my hands—give me leave to assure you it was a Cordial to my then drooping spirits—I scarce know what to say in respect to the late retreat, one thing however I firmly believe that Genl St. Clair will with the Candid & impartiall still be considered the Great Soldier Honest Man even after the most narrow scrutiny—With regard to a certain General who was not on the Spot—the Clamors of the People are great indeed & in case of an attack from the Enemy God only knows the consequence.—The army are now at a place called Moses's Creek having Evacuated Fort Edward, the militia as usual desert by Regiments, if this part of the Continent is really to be defended, it must be in my humble opinion by a considerable supply of Continental Troops —. A strong party of the enemy are at Castleton in the Grants with Govorner Skene at their Head cajoling the Inhabitants & I fear meet with too much success—Col: Warner is also there with a party of Militia to watch their motions— In Short My Dear General I look upon our present situation to be a critical one indeed, but I still hope your Warm prayer will be heard & our Rightious Cause not suffered to perish because Sinners are concerned in the defence of it — . Your Friends are well and at Camp which I left yesterday. The Indians are daily scalping around the camp even below Fort Edward .— I send this by Express by return if your business would admit, I should be happy to receive a line from you.— My most affectionate compliments to your good Family & believe me to be

"My Dear General your
"much obliged & most humble
"Servt
"JON^N POTTS.

"ALBANY *July* 28th 1777.

"*P: S:* I fortunately saved the bulk of my medicine, have my Hospital here, another at Saratoga & the third at Camp, the army are very Healthy, the whole of the Sick & wounded not exceeding 200.

"*July* 28th 8 *o'clock A: M:*

"A letter from Col: Lewis this moment arrived mentions that last evening a party of the Enemy of about 1000 attacked our Picquet near Fort Edward of 150 men drove them in Kill'd five men among whom is a Lieut: they also Kill'd a young Lady Dr McCrea's Sister all of whom they scalped & butchered."* (Gates' MSS., p. 39.)

The scene having now changed, the English aurhorities are now able to contribute something to the history of Fort George.

It appears that, when St. Clair's retreat of July 6th became known, Major Yates, who was in command at Fort George, marched away to Fort Edward with seven hundred men, carrying his baggage and stores, and setting the fort on fire. This took place July 16th. Burgoyne, who was then moving victoriously southward, thus writes of the affair:

"The garrison of Fort George in manifest danger of being cut off by the direct movement from Skenesborough to Hudson's River, took the measure I expected of abandoning the Fort, and burning the vessels, thereby leaving the lake entirely free. A detachment of the King's Troops from Ticonderoga, which I had ordered to be ready for that event, with a great embarkation of provisions, passed the lake on the same day that I took possession of this communication by land."

General Schuyler justified the abandonment of Fort George; on which point Washington, when writing, suspended his own opinion, remarking that others had informed him, "that a spirited, brave, judicious officer, with two or three hundred good men, together with the armed vessels you have built, would retard Burgoyne's passage across the Lake for a considerable time, if not render it impracticable, and oblige him to take a more difficult and circuitous route."

To this Schuyler replies:

"The fort was part of an unfinished bastion of an intended fortification. The bastion was closed at the gorge. In it was a barrack capable

---

* It is, perhaps, hardly necessary to delay here to remark that the whole question in regard to the death of this unfortunate young woman, is one involved in doubt. Whether she was killed by accident or design is not clear to all.

of containing between thirty and fifty men; without ditch, without wall, without cistern; without any picket to prevent an enemy from running over the wall. So small, as not to contain above one hundred and fifty men, commanded by ground greatly overlooking it, and within point blank shot; and so situated that five hundred men may lie between the bastion and the Lake, without being seen from this *extremely* defensible fortress. Of vessels built there, one was afloat and tolerably fitted; the others still upon the stocks; but, if the two had been upon the water, they would have been of but little use, without rigging and guns." ("Washington's Writings," Vol. IV, p. 494.).

This was clearly a time of very great depression and distress. Governeur Morris, in writing to John Jay in regard to the trials of Valley Forge in 1780, suddenly turns from the spectacle, saying, "But I have seen Fort George in the summer of 1777." ("Life," Vol. I, p. 154.)

The air was filled with rumors, and the wagons sent to Fort George to bring away stores were reported "cut off," which aroused Schuyler, who marched to the rescue with five hundred men. This episode is thus told:

"HEAD QUARTERS, FORT EDWARD, *July 15th*, 1777.

"GENTLEMEN—A report having been propagated here a few hours ago, that a number of wagons, which had been sent this morning to Fort George to remove some stores from that place, had been cut off by a large party of the enemy's Indians, General Schuyler immediately marched with a body of troops towards Fort George. On his way he received a letter from Colonel Ashley, who commands at the Five Mile Run, of which the enclosed is a copy; by that it seems the enemy's numbers must have been very inconsiderable, as we had near a hundred wagons on the road, and we cannot learn that they have been molested.

"I am, gent. respectfully,
"Your most humble servant,
"JOHN LANSING, Junr."
("J. N. Y. Prov. Congress," Vol. II, p. 112.)

July 16, Governeur Morris writes from Fort Edward: "Fort Ann is abandoned, & Fort George will be so by tomorrow this time, if not sooner taken." He says, also, in a postscript: "If we get our stores from Lake George, & accomplish a safe retreat to this place * * our affairs will wear a more smiling aspect."

The next day he wrote again from Saratoga:

"I left Fort Edward with Gen. Schuyler at noon, and shall return thither some time to-morrow morning. Fort George was destroyed yesterday afternoon, previous to which, the provisions, stores, batteaux, &c. were removed, and this morning about ten o'clock the last of them passed us about three miles to the northward of Fort Edward, at which place all the troops from the lake have arrived, and these, together with some others, from our advanced post towards Fort George; about twelve hundred, perhaps more, are somewhat farther advanced upon the road to Fort Anne. The enemy have not yet made any motion that we know of, nor indeed can they make any of consequence until they shall have procured carriages, and then they may find it rather difficult to come this way, if proper care be taken to prevent them from procuring forage. For this purpose, I shall give it as my opinion to the General, whenever he asks it, to break up all the settlements upon our northern frontier, to drive off the cattle, secure or destroy the forage, &c; and also to destroy the saw mills. These measures, harsh as they may seem, are, I am confident, absolutely necessary. They ought undoubtedly to be taken with prudence, and temperately carried into execution. But I will venture to say, that if we lay it down as a maxim, never to contend for ground but in the last necessity, to leave nothing but a wilderness to the enemy, their progress must be impeded by obstacles which it is not in human nature to surmount; and then, unless we have with our usual good nature, built posts for *their* defence, they must at the approach of winter retire to the place from whence they at first set out. The militia from the eastward come in by degrees, and I expect we shall soon be in force to carry on the *petite guerre* to advantage, provided always, Burgoyne attempts to annoy us, for it is pretty clear that we cannot get at him." ("New York Congress," Vol. II, p. 508.)

The garrison at Fort George had a somewhat narrow escape, as appears from a minute dated, in camp at Fort Edward, Aug. 6. 1777:

"Very fortunately for the garrison at Fort George, they had passed this place about an hour before our arrival; had they been that much later, they must have been inevitably cut off." ("Anbury's Travels," Vol. I, p. 363.)

Burgoyne clearly aimed at the capture of the garrison, as, on the 11th of July, he wrote to Sir Guy Carlton:

"My present purpose, Sir, is to get a sufficient number of Gunboats upon the Lake George to scour that Lake as expeditiously as possible, to support them them with a proper force to attack Fort George on that side, while with the main army, as soon as refreshed and supplied, I attack Fort Edward from hence [Skenesborough] and thereby cut off the communication from Albany to Fort George, & consequently prevent the succour or retreat of that garrison." ("Burgoyne's Report," Ap. XLII.)

Evidently Burgoyne considered this an important point. We find that the enemy had accurate knowledge of everything of consequence in relation to the positions and the fortifications.

Fort George, wrongly called "Fort Edward," is thus described in Riedesel's papers of 1777, at a time when the Americans were still in posssssion:

"1st. The citadel has been recently repaired and provided with two nine pounders. It contains, also, twelve cannon, which are not yet mounted. Barracks for 1,000 men lie within twenty yards east of it.

"2d. Close to the shore is a large magazine in which there is an abundance of provisions.

"3d. To the west of this magazine, where Fort William Henry formerly stood, is a large hospital, a building of great dimensions, & used for the sick from Fort Carrillon.* This is said to be surrounded by palisades, and to have a small redoubt on the hill south of it. A strong guard is posted here every night. The rebels at Fort George are very busy cutting down trees & carrying them to the shore, to be used in the construction of six strong vessels on the lake. A so-called Commodore Wyncoop, is said still to be in command at this post; only one regiment, it is further said, remains here during the summer; but as yet there are only 400 men there. There is also considerable scarcity of ammunition." ("Riedesel's Journal," Vol. I, p. 295.)

As Burgoyne himself relates, a British force passed over Lake George and took possession of the fort on the day it was deserted by the Americans. Whoever may have *commanded* this detachment at the time, Colonel Anstruther appears to have held Fort George, where he afterwards received the Baroness Riedesel,† the wife of the general, when on her way to join her husband in Burgoyne's army.

The materials for this period are exceedingly scanty, as no one appears to have been interested in compiling notes.

---

* The French name of Ticonderoga, meaning a chime, and given on account of the music ot the Fall, which are of considerable height.

† The Baroness says, in her Journal: "The following day passed Ticonderoga, and about noon arrived at Fort George, where we dined with Colonel Anstruther, an exceedingly good and amiable man, who commands the 62d regiment. In the afternoon we seated ourselves in a calash, & reached Fort Edward on the same day, which was the 14th of August." (Munsell's Reprint, p. 91.)

CHAPTER VI.

URNING AGAIN to "Riedesel's Journal" we take the following: "On the 15th July General Riedesel was ordered to Ticonderoga to superintend the removal of Ships to Lake George. Of the two regiments yet remaining at Ticonderoga—the 62d English and Prince Frederick's—one half of each, under the command of Colonel Anstruther and Major Von Hiller, was to cover the removal." (*Ibid*, p. 124.)

"26 July. The Ships & baggage were to be transported by Canadians to Lake George, & thence to Fort Edward on the Hudson River." (*Ibid*, p. 124.)

July 31. "General Phillips—having accomplished the removal of the Stores and artillery from Ticonderoga—had arrived at Fort George, and was busily engaged in building a road from that fort to Fort Edward." (*Ibid*, p. 125.)

"Camp near Fort Edward. Aug 5. 1777.

"An Officer and 20 men with Non Commission Officers in proportion from the Line will conduct all the prisoners taken from the Enemy to Fort George, to-morrow morning." ("Burgoyne's Order Book," p. 64.)

"Camp near Fort Edward. Aug. 6 1777.

"Four companies will embark at Fort George in the First return Boats, and the remaining four companies are to wait for the boats that bring the 62d Regiment from Ticonderoga." (*Ibid*, p. 68.)

Aug. 9th. "Brigadier Powell was ordered to take with him the 53d Regiment and relieve Brigadier Hamilton at Ticonderoga: at the same time the 62d. was ordered to rejoin the army. The company of Canadian Militia, under Boucherville, was to remain at Fort George." (*Ibid*, p. 126.)

Aug. 17. Burgoyne "entrusted to Riedesel the duty of maintaining communication with Fort Anne and Fort George."

Aug. 31. Burgoyne says, though with some misapprehension in regard to the facts of the case, that,

"Regarding Fort George, it is my intention to leave there four companies of the 47th Regiment, two of which will occupy the fort, & the remainder the island three miles distant from the land. I take it for granted that the fort is safe against surprise, no matter how strong the attacking party may be. In case of assault, the garrison can still retreat through the open ditch, to the island, whither the enemy can never go, being destitute of ships, while we, on the contrary, have gunboats." (*Ibid*, p. 274.)

The officer placed in command, in accordance with this resolution, as we shall see further on, was Lieutenant Irwine.

Sept. 1st. All the heavy baggage of Burgoyne's army was sent back to Ticonderoga. "Those articles, however, which might be most needed, were only sent back as far as Diamond Island in Lake George—seven [three?] miles from Fort George—that they might be close at hand in case of need. At the same time two companies of the 47 Regiment were sent with them as a garrison; only thirty men & one officer being left at Fort George, as the communication with that lake was to be given up for the present. In pursuance of this plan the two companies of the 53d. Regiment, which had been hitherto stationed at Fort George, were sent to Ticonderoga to reinforce that post." ("Riedesel's Journal," p. 134.)

On Sept. 3d, "Riedesel left Fort George for the purpose of expediting the transports for the army."

Sept. 10, Burgoyne again writes, "The last [secret] orders have been given to have nothing remain in Fort George. The last of the wagons will accordingly pass Fort Edward Either tomorrow evening or Friday morning." In the same letter, he says, that General St. Leger had been obliged to retreat to Oswego, and was expected at the lake, adding, "I have sent him orders as to the necessary measures of precaution he is to take upon arriving on the island at the lower end of Lake George." (*Ibid*, p. 275.)

Sept. 11th, General Riedesel "was very much occupied in transporting stores from Fort George to Fort Edward, whence they were carried down the Hudson." ("Journal," Vol. 1, p. 138.)

In the meanwhile, a movement was planned by the American General Lincoln to make an important raid upon Burgoyne's rear. The plan of the enterprise is sketched in a letter from Lincoln to General Gates:

"Pawlet *September* 14*th*. 1777.
"Dear General,   noon.

"I just now received your favor of yesterdays date. By a scout which hath been near Fort Edward, and from one of the Inhabitants in that neighbourhood, I have a confirmation of the enemy's movements mentioned in your letter. I think it is most probable, their design is on your post; however, I will keep the most watchful eye over them, and, if possible, prevent a surprise.

"On being informed, by almost every person who came in, as well as by letter you inclosed me from General Palmer, of the weak state of Ticonderoga; and also advices that a considerable number of our men were prisoners in the enemy's hands, and kept at Lake George landing, under a very small guard; at which place the enemy had a large Magazine of stores; and supposing a movement that way, would perfectly coincide with the original design, of my being here; vizt. if possible, to divide and distract the enemy;—was induced yesterday, with the advice of the officers, to send Colonel Brown, with five hundred men, to the landing at Lake George, to relieve the prisoners, and distroy the stores there,—the same number of men under Colonel Johnson, to mount independence; the latter to give a divertion to the enemy, while the former should execute his commission; and if an opportunity should offer, without risking too much, to push for mount independence, while Colonel Browne would attempt Ticonderoga—and further, to amuse, and divide the enemy, by attacking their out posts &c.—alike number of men were sent under Colonel Woodbridge, to skeensboro, thence to Fort Ann, and on towards fort Edward.—I hope these movements will meet your approbation; I should have mentioned ye design before, and not put the plan in execution, without your advice, could I have been sure the information would not have fallen into the hands of the enemy.— I suppose you intended to hint to me your apprehension of danger in this way, and that I must be cautious what I wrote, when in the close of your favor of the 10th instant you say: 'I desire you will not fail, frequently to acquaint me with your movements, and, as far as is prudent, with your designs.'

"I am dear General with sincere regard
               "Your most obedient and humble servant.
                                                                            "B: Lincoln.
"The Honble Major Genl Gates."   (Gates' MSS.)

At Ticonderoga Colonel Brown accomplished considerable; even as when he first proved his courage at the capture of the place, May 10, 1775, by bravely supporting Benedict Arnold, who was the first man to enter the fort. At the beginning of this the second attack, Brown was again successful, but, in the end, he was obliged to abandon the enterprise, and retire with his trophies and the American prisoners whom he had succeeded in liberating. But not yet satisfied, he resolved to make an attack first upon Diamond Island, and afterwards upon Fort

George, using for this purpose the vessels captured from the British at the north end of the lake, an event that Burgoyne never anticipated. The results of this movement are given by Burgoyne, who writes:

"On the 24th instant, the enemy upon Lake George attacked Diamond Island in two divisions. Captain Aubrey* and two companies of the 47th regiment had been posted at that island from the time the army passed the Hudson River, as a better security for the stores at the south end of Lake George than Fort George, which is on the continent, and not tenable against artillery and numbers. The enemy were repulsed by Captain Aubrey with great loss, and pursued by the gunboats under his command, to the east shore, where two of their principal vessels were retaken, together with all the cannon. They had just time to set fire to the other batteaux, and retreated over the mountain."†

Brown arranged the plan of the attack with skill, but the artillery of the British was too powerful for the sides of his little lake craft, and he was obliged to retreat, though with a trifling, instead of "great loss," as Burgoyne phrased it.

It must be remarked, however, as a singular fact, that the fullest published account of the "Life of Colonel Brown," an able and meritorious officer, makes no allusion to this affair at Diamond Island, but represents that he was ordered to Fort George to release the American prisoners there, when the prisoners, whom Colonel Brown happily liberated, were confined at Ticonderoga.

As an account of the history of this campaign is not included in the plan of these "Notes," it will be sufficient to say that, eventually, defeat crowned the efforts of Burgoyne, and his army was surrendered to General Gates.‡

The small force of British that now remained on Lake George after the surrender of their chief withdrew to Ticonderoga, where General Powell held command.

Nov. 1. Samuel Herrick, colonel commanding at Pawlet, attacked Powell in his stronghold at Mount Independence, with the following characteristic letter:

"Pawlet Nov' 1' 1777.

"Sir:

"By the time this comes to hand, I hope you will have recovered from the surprise with which you have been repeatedly effected since my

---

* Thomas Aubrey, second son of Sir Thomas Aubrey, of Glanborganshire, entered the army as ensign in 1762, and served in Florida. He was at the Battle of Bunker Hill, and was made a major in 1782, and afterwards rose to the rank of colonel. He died, January 15, 1814.

† "Burgoyne's Report," App. LIII. For the *full* account of this transaction, with the original reports, *see* the author's paper on "The Battle of Diamond Island," now about being published in a separate form.

‡ Two days before the surrender of Burgoyne, Sept. 15, being then at Fort Edward, David How says, in his "Diary:" "This morning our Scouts Brought in upwards of 50 Indians that were made prisoners Yesterday Near Fort George—They had With them Silver & Gold And a Number of Blankets And other Valuable Bagege." ("Diary," p. 48.)

correspondence with you—You Impute my conduct to Ignorance of the rules of War, I hope Sir I have not been Guilty of Ill manners

"if you please sir, I am ready to conclude the Trifling correspondence with you provided you will Quit the Ground immediately, on which you now pretend to teach me military rules, Otherwise I shall endeavour to convince you at the Head of my GREEN MOUNTAIN BOYS, That your dominion is but Temporary

"I am sincerely sir
"Your most Humble Servt
"SAML HERRICK Colo Comd
"To the Honorable Brigadier Genl POWEL Commanding at mount independence." ("Gates' MSS.)

General Powell, however, does not appear to have been greatly alarmed by the "Green Mountain Boys," whom he estimated by his own ideas of value; yet, when he found that he could no further support the sinking cause of the King by holding his position, he retired to the North. Herrick, however, supposed that General Powell believed him "serious," and that the belief caused a "precipitate" retreat. Probably what the general feared was another *letter*. But we must allow Herrick to tell his own story.

"POWLET *November* 14th 1777.
"SIR

"I have the pleasure to inform you, that the Enemy have abandoned Tyconderoga Mount Independence &c on sattarday Last After dimolishing all the Fortifications, Bridges, Burning all the Houses, and destroying all stores Cannon &c. which they could not bring off,—their retreat was precipitate inded, as appears by many circumstances.

"A few days before I was informed by deserters that their shipping and a number of Boats were Loaded for St. Johns, who had orders to return immediately to fetch more Loading .— About that time I ordered Capt. Hemn Allen with 60 Rangers down to Lake Champlain with orders to Take two Armed vessels by stratagem, and to secure what provisions, Forage &c. he could, Capt. Allen was join'd by Capt. Ln at Rutland, and a considerable number of the Inhabitants & hunters a few days after which enlarged Capt. Allens ditachments to about 200 men.

"I suppose they had not yet recovered from the surprise which my letter of Nov 1st occasioned them, when Capt Allens detachment was, discovered on the Lake a few days After, which made them suppose I was serious [*sic*] in my hinted projects, and being afraid, that their retreat would be cut off at the Narrows, they immediately began their retreat on the 3d Instant and finished the whole on Sattarday Last,

"Major Wait is gone with 75 men to take possession and to secure Stores, Cattle, Horses, &c boats, if the enemy have left any. Capt. Allen is now harrassing the Enemies rear, endeavoring to take some scatring boats.

"The Coast is now clear and the season is far advanced and nothing more is to be feared from the Enemy in this Quarter til Spring."
* * * * *   (Gates' MSS., Vol. II, p. 5.)

Military criticism is the proper work of soldiers, and yet it may be allowable to advert briefly to the reasons that led Burgoyne to choose the route by South Bay in preference to that of Fort George. Here, therefore, let us insert Burgoyne's own defence. He writes:

"Question has been made by those who began at this period to arraign my military conduct, whether it would not have been more expedient for the purpose of rapidity, to have fallen back to Ticonderoga, in order to take the convenient route by Lake George, than to have persevered in the laborious & difficult course by land to Fort Edward. My motives for preferring the latter were these: I considered not only the general impressions which a retrograde motion is apt to make upon the minds of both enemies & friends, but also, that the natural conduct of the Enemy in that case would be to remain at Fort George, as their retreat could not then be cut off, in order to oblige me to open trenches, and consequently to delay me, and in the meantime they would have destroyed the road from Fort George to Fort Edward. On the other hand, by persisting to penetrate by the short cut from Fort Anne, of which I was then master, to Fort Edward, though it was attended with great labor, and many alert situations, the troops were improved in the very essential point of wood service; I effectully dislodged the Enemy from Fort George without a blow; and seeing me master of one communication, they did not think it worth while to destroy the other." ("Burgoyne's Report," p. 12.)

It is clear, from what he says about opening trenches, that he knew nothing of the real indefensibility of Fort George. Again, he writes to show how he gained time:

"I therefore shall add only two short remarks; the one, that the fact of gaining considerable time by allotting the whole service of the water craft to the transport of provision & stores over Lake George, instead of employing great part of it for the transport of troops, is incontestably proved by the evidence of Captain Money and Lieutenant Colonel Kingston: the other, that to have reached Fort Edward with the troops sooner than the 29th of July (the day that the first embarkation of provisions reached Fort George) would not only have been useless but also highly impolitic." (*Ibid*, p. 97.)

Still further, he declares that, in case he had moved his whole force over Lake George,

"To maintain the communication with Fort George during such a movement, so as to be supplied by daily degrees at a distance, continually increasing, was an obvious impossiblity." (*Ibid*, App. XXII.)

In the course of the official inquiry into Burgoyne's military policy, the following questions were put to the Earl of Balcarras:

"*Q.* Had the army proceeded to Fort George by Ticonderoga and Lake George, might not the enemy have remained at Fort George till the trenches were opened, and have still had their retreat secure?

"*A.* That is a matter of opinion upon speculation.

"*Q.* Do you think that the British army, being well provided with the artillery, was a probable reason for their not defending entrenchments?

"*A.* The reason they did not defend their entrenchments was, that they always marched out of them and attacked us."

To the first question the answer is an idle one, while the reply to the second is simply pert. Every one who *knew* anything of Fort George knew that a fox could have run over its walls. The idea of a siege would have made the commander smile. It is true that Washington himself was "informed"* that a brave commander could have held the fort, and delayed the advance of the British, but what shall we say of his informant?

In regard to the allegation that the Americans were accustomed to march out of their intrenchments to attack the British, we need only to remember that such was simply not the case.

The misfortunes of a military commander always inspire hostile critics with an astuteness that is remarkable and a wisdom that is profound. Still we must do justice to King George by quoting his declaration, written *before* the advance of Burgoyne, wherein he says:

"If possible, possession must be taken of Lake George, and nothing but an absolute impossibility of succeeding in this can be an excuse for proceeding by South Bay & Skenesborough."†

The seat of war having been removed by the surrender of Burgoyne, and the return of the remaining British forces to Canada, Fort George remained in quiet until 1780. The life of the little garrison, though dull enough, no doubt, in fact, would now, if it had been placed on record, afforded many incidents of interest to the historian. But the record we do not possess, though many an old diary bearing on the subject may now be reposing amid the dust of ancient alcoves and garrets, waiting to be drawn forth to light by the antiquary's hand.

Still the war was not destined to end without further adventures, for, in the autumn of 1780, Fort George suddenly came out once more into public notice.

Impelled by the desire to recover three barrels of silver-plate, then buried in the cellar of his house at Johnstown, and encouraged, perhaps, by the prospective results of the treason of Benedict Arnold, Sir John Johnson threaded his way down from Canada through the gorgeous

---

* *See* p. 36, *ante.*   † Albermarle's "Memoirs of the Marquis of Rockingham," Vol. II. p. 331.

October forests, bore off his treasure, and retired northward again, pursued by Governor Clinton, and marking his line of invasion with flames and smoke. Major Carlton likewise improved the occasion to come up Champlain and strike a blow at Forts Ann and George. The first-mentioned post fell on October 10th, and Fort George met the same fate on the following day. But as we have in the "Garrison Orders" of the few days previous some glimpses of the condition of things, let us give them here:

"GARRISON ORDERS FORT GEORGE
"Septr 26 178–

"Every Non Commissioned officer and Soldier that has drew Bayonet Scabords and Belts from the public are to return them to Public Store—
"The Commanding officers of Companies to see the above articles Colected and the Regimental Quarter master to Recpt for the Same—
"JOHN CHIPMAN Capt Comdt^t.

"GARRISON ORDERS FORT GEORGE
"Octob^r 2 1780—

"Where as Complaint is maid by the Adgn^t and Sargn^t Magor of the great Difficulty they meet with in giting the men out the Perade in consiquence of which there are to direct that the Revile is Beat every morning at break of day when every officer Non Commissioned officer and soldier are to attend the perade, except one officers S$_{a}$rv^{nt} to each room—the men are also ordered to keep their arms and accoutrements in good order and in such position that they can lay their hands upon them in the dark and if ocation Calls be ready for action in a moment— They are also to observe to be on the perade on every call of the drum without the least delay—The Sargeant of the gard is to awake the drumer every morning—
"The Commanding officer Expects these orders will be complied with in the strictest sence of the word. and who ever disobeys may expect the severest punishment.—
"JOHN CHIPMAN Capt Comd^t

"GARRISON ORDERS FORT GEORGE.
"Octr 8th 1780—

"Court Martial to set immediately to such prisoners as shall be brought before them
"THOMAS SILL is President
"Ens^n GRANT } Members
"d LIGHTHALL }
"The Court to set where the President shall appoint.
"P   JOHN CHIPMAN Capt Comd^t

"The Court Convened and being duly sworn proceeded to the tryal of Corp^{ll} John Fretcher of Capt Wollcotts Company confined Neglect ot duty—Pleads not guilty The Court after hearing the evidence finds him guilty; and sentince him to be reduced to a private Sentinal and do duty as such.

"Tho⁸ Sill Pris^dt

"The above Judgment approved of and ordered to be Complied with this evening at Rool Call—

"John Chipman Capt Comd^r.

"Garrison Orders Fort George.

"Oct^br 11 1778

"Sir as it is reported to me that their is a small party of savages near Bloddy pond, you will immediately take Forty Eight men, officers included and Proseed on the main road until you make discoveries of them, keeping a Suffiscient advance and Flank gards in Such a manner as to prevent being surrounded. if you find a large party you will Emmediately Retreat to the fort except they should be savages only in which case you will attack and immediately Charge upon them—"

("Hist. Mag.," 1867, p. 378.)

But here the garrison orders suddenly came to an end, and the fort, with its single mounted gun, sooh changed masters.

CHAPTER VII.

INVASIONS like the so-called "Northern Invasion" had often been predicted, and Fort George, as we have seen, had often been threatened. Now, however, the act longed for by the Tories took place. On the 11th of October, ignorant of the surrender of Fort Ann, and mistaking the advancing force of Major Carlton for a handful of roving savages, Captain Chipman sent out a party to reconnoitre. Meeting the enemy, they advanced to the attack, and were defeated, Captain Sill and two ensigns being killed, while the rest, with the exception of an ensign and fourteen men, surrendered. Those who thus escaped fled to the fort, which Carlton quickly surrounded. Resistance being useless, Fort George soon capitulated to the enemy, obtaining honorable terms.

But, notwithstanding the commander acted with all the bravery and circumspection that the case demanded, there was not wanting an accuser to misrepresent the circumstances.

Concerning this affair, Governor Clinton reported to General Washington, Oct. 30, that:

"The little post and garrison of Fort Ann, appeared to me to have been surrendered through treachery or cowardice. Capt Chipman, the commanding officer of Fort George, having on the first alarm sent out his whole garrison, (supposing the enemy to consist of only ab^t 30 Indians and tories), except 14 men obtained a very honorable capitulation, before he could be induced to surrender." ("Letters to Washington," Vol. III, p. 133.)

Aspersions like these very naturally brought out a defence from Captain Chipman, and he accordingly addressed the following letter to the public press:*

---

* This communication appears to have escaped the attention of those who have written on this subject.

"Mr. GREEN,

"The Singularity of the Misfortunes which happened at Fort George, on the 11th of October last, will justify a Desire that you will publish the following just Narration of the Circumstances of that unhappy Affair through the Channel of your paper.

"In the Beginning of October last, having the Command at Fort George, I was informed by my Scouts from the North End of Lake George, that they had discovered two Sail of the Enemy's Vessels at Anchor at Crown Point; which Intelligence, though nothing unusual, I communicated to Colonel Malcom, Commanding Officer in the Northern Department.

"The Enemy's Force consisting of 800 British, one Company of Yagers, 175 Indians and 200 Tories, under the Command of Major Carleton, gained a rapid Passage from Ticonderoga to the Head of South Bay, in the Night of the 8th of October, detaching a Party to return with their Boats to the Carrying-Place into Lake George, in Order to transport their Howitzer, Shells, &c. across that Lake to the Fort, which though dignified with that Term is but an unfinished Angle of the Intended Fort.*

"Monday the 8th of October, Capt. Sherwood, who commanded at Fort Ann, (a small Stockade, seven Miles South of the Head of South Bay, 20 E. N. E. from Fort George, and 14 from Fort Edward, garrisoned with two Lieutenants and seventy-five Men) was informed by his Scouts of the Approach of the Enemy, which Intelligence he Immediately communicated to Col. Henry Livingston, who commanded at Fort Edward; but Col. Livingston not forwarding the Intelligence to me, I was totally in the Dark with respect to the Enemy's Incursion into the Country against Fort Ann and the Vicinity.

"Tuesday the 10th, about Noon, Col. Livingston was inform'd by two Gentlemen who had occasionally rode out and narrowly escaped being taken, of the Enemy's having captured Fort Ann, and were making a rapid Progress through Kingsbury, burning and destroying all before them: Expresses were dispatched from Fort Edward upon this second Intelligence into the Country, but none to Fort George, altho' the Communication was open 'till 3 o'Clock in the Afternoon. Upon my being informed of the two Vessels before-mention'd at Crown-Point, I thought it necessary to keep a strict Eye upon them, and accordingly dispatched a Batteau in the Night to the North-End of Lake George, to watch their Motions, not knowing of their Troops having penetrated the Country by the Rout of South-Bay. This Boat went within eight Miles of the Landing, and† to Reconnoitre the Enemy, when they discovered the Party with the Howitzer, &c. fearing for Fort George; my Party finding their Retreat thus cut off wisely made their Escape by Land.

---

* *See* Schuyler's "Letter," p. 36, *ante.*
† The letters are blurred here and undecipherable. Copies of the paper are scarce.

"Wednesday the 11th. The Garrison having been two Days without Provisions, I sent an Express to Fort Edward to have some forwarded, but he returned, having discovered a Party of Indians near Bloody-Pond, about a Mile and Half from the Fort. Thus situated without Provision, Artillery, and but a small Quantity of Ammunition, I thought it most advisable to reconnoitre this Party, with a View of falling upon the best Method of saving the small Garrison, and accordingly issued the following Order, from which I hoped some Advantage would arise either by clearing the Road of the Savages or of protecting any Convoy of Provision that might be coming to the Fort.

"GARRISON ORDERS.

"FORT GEORGE, *October* 11th, 1780

"SIR,

"As it is reported to me that there is a small Party of Savages near Bloody-Pond, you will immediately take the Command of a Party of forty-eight Men, Officers included, and proceed on *main Road* until you make Discoveries of them, keeping sufficient advanced and flank Guards in such a Manner as to prevent being surrounded; if you find a large Party you will immediately retreat to the Fort except they should be Savages only, in which Case you will immediately attack and charge upon them.*

"JOHN CHIPMAN, Capt. Commandant.

"To Capt. THOMAS SILL.

"Capt. Sill immediately marched, but unfortunately taking a Rout different from his Orders, he passed the Enemy on their Approach, and on his Return fell upon their Rear, which effectually prevented a Possibility of his Return to the Fort, and reduced him to the desperate Alternative of attacking a Body of *at least thirty to one*, or to march off through the Woods and expose himself to the infamous Reflections of Ignorance and Detraction; like brave Men they unanimously agreed on the Former and formed their Line, advancing (each Officer in command of his proper Section) near a Mile upon the Enemy, when they formed and were instantaniously attacked by this handful of brave Men who soon forced them to give way, and advanced on with charged Bayonets; but their Numbers being now known to the Enemy they soon surrounded and killed or took the whole, except Ensign Grant with 14 Men who made their Escape, and wisely kept clear of the Garrison, Capt. Sill and two Ensigns fell in the Action, and the Enemy immediately invested the Fort, and were opposed from the Wall by a six Pounder (being the only Piece of Ordnance mounted in the Fort) and 15 small Arms until they summoned a Surrender, which was granted after obtaining the following Terms, which I have the Confidence to declare I am not ashamed of, and could not have expected better if I had ten Times the Number.

---

* This is the same order already quoted, revised for the printer.

"This, Mr. Printer is a plain State of the Facts, and it will immediately appear to every One that the want of Men, Artillery, Ammunition and Provision is Cause sufficient for the Surrender of tenable Forts, much more for the wretched Production of a cantrous Jebb, and that the sending Capt. Sill was the only Step that could produce Advantage, by bringing in the Provision had it been upon the Road, or by making such Discoveries as would have authorized an Evacuation; but when Orders are disobeyed, it is not surprising that Plans are not executed. I obtained my Parole of Maj. Carleton until the 15th of next May, which has been a Matter of Cavil to the busy Propagators of unmerited Abuse and the pittyful Retailers of groundless Slander.

"I am, Sir,
"Your most humble Servant,
"JOHN CHIPMAN,
"Col. Warner's Regiment."

("Connecticut Gazette," Feb. 16, 1781.)

To this he appends the articles of capitulation which were revised. Therefore we give them *verbatim:*

"Articles of Capitulation between Major Carleton, commanding a detachment of the King's troops, and Capt. Chipman, Commanding at Fort George.

"*Article 1st* The Troops of the garrison to surrender themselves prisoners of war.

"*Article 2nd* That the women & children be permitted to return to their homes, with two waggons & their baggage.

"*Article 3d* Each officer shall be allowed their servants

"*Article 4th* No Indian to enter the fort until a British detachment takes possession of the fort.

"*Article 5th* Major Carleton passes his honor that no levies on the fort shall be lost, nor any person to be molested.

"*Article 6th* Each Soldier to carry his Knapsack

"*Article 7th* Ensign Barrett shall be permitted to return home with his family & the regimental books, on giving his parole to Major Carleton

"JOHN CHIPMAN, Capt Coms 2d Battalion.
"JAMES KIRKMAN, Lt. 29th Regt.
"WM JOHNSTON, Lt. 47th Regt.
"CHR CARLTON, Major 29th Regt, &., &., &."

("Almon's Remembrancer," 1781, p. 81.)

To this may properly be added the return of the killed, wounded, and prisoners taken at Forts Ann and George, the 10th and 11th of October, 1780: "Killed, 1 Captain, 2 Lieutenants, 1 Ensign, 23 privates.—Wounded, 1 Lieutenant, one private.—Prisoners, 2 captains, 2 Lieutenants, 114 privates."

The English loss is given as follows:

"Return of the Killed and wounded of the detachment under the command of Major Carleton, the 11th of October, 1780.

"34th regiment, 1 private Killed, 1 Sergeant and 1 private wounded.— King's rangers, 1 private Killed.—Major Jessop's corps, 1 private wounded.— Indians, 1 Killed, 1 wounded." (*Ibid,* p. 82.)

To make the documentory portion of our story complete, we must add some extracts from the correspondence of Col. Gansevoort with Major Carleton. The former says:

"A certain James Van Deusen, who deserted from our service to you, and who, since you were on this side of the lake, has stolen back into the country, has been apprehended, & will suffer death as a deserter. He confesses that after the recontre near Fort George, with some of Col. Warner's men and your party, in which one of the Indians was Killed, your Indians, in cold blood, Scalped one of Warner's men alive, tormented him a considerable time, & afterwards cut his throat—and all this in your presence."

To this Major Carleton replied:

"I should have expected Captain Chapnan [Chipman] would have given a flat contradiction to James Van Deusen's confession. No prisoner was scalped, or tortured alive. I saved the lives of several of the prisoners, who were neither stripped nor insulted in the smallest degree when the affair was over. I heard of one man being killed after he was taken during the firing, owing to a dispute between the two Indians, of different villages who had taken him. He was either a negro or a Stockbridge Indian I believe. & he would not suffer himself to be conducted to the British guard by a loyalist officer." (Stone's "Brant," Vol, II, p. 134.)

In regard to the manner in which the capture was accomplished, Governor Haldimand wrote, Oct. 25th, commending Major Carleton, saying: "The Secrecy and despatch with which this detachment penetrated, prevented any opposition of consequence on the part of the enemy; and on the 10th and 11th instant, the garrisons of Fort Ann & Fort George surrendered prisoners of war." ("London Gazette" in "Almon's Remembrancer," 1781, p. 81.)

It will be seen that Captain Chipman was expecting an enemy by the way of Lake George, but was misled, and that, after the capture of Fort Ann, he was not apprised of the fact. The information sent to others did not reach him.

Oct. 13th, Col. Malcom wrote to Gen. Van Rensselaer that "a very considerable body of the Enemy appeared on Tuesday at Fort Ann, which was instantly given up by Capt Sherwood. They came on to the river & burnt a number of houses about Fort Edward. Yesterday they returned towards Lake George." (Hough's "Northern Invasion," p. 93.)

The day previous, Stephen Lush, communicating with Governor Clinton, says "Colo Livingston writes, that his intelligence is, that Carleton with his party are now at Fort George, and are to be joined by a party from Ballstown under command of Sir John [Carleton]: and that he [Col. Livingston] means if he can, with safety to his post, march to the relief of Fort George." (*Ibid*, p. 90.)

But though there was considerable alarm, nothing was actually done to stay the progress of the invaders; and finally, Hall's "Poughkeepsie Journal," of Oct. 16, announced to the public:

"We hear from the northward, that a considerable body of British Troops, Indians and Tories from Canada, by way of Lake Champlain, have taken our posts at Fort George & Fort Ann, with the small garrison; and that the enemy are still burning & ravaging the country, in the neighborhood of Fort Edward."

Little blame can, on the whole, be thrown upon the commander at Fort George, especially as General Schuyler himself, writing the previous April, thought that the prospect of danger from the enemy was small.

Governor Clinton appears to have taken a very active part in the defence of this year, and May 29th was at Fort George, having come thus far in pursuit of Sir John Johnson's band of marauders. Yet, when the danger was really at hand, no adequate force was prepared to meet it, and thus fort George fell, the English invaders, on the whole, earning the commendation that General Haldimand bestowed.

In regard to the disposition of the garrison of Fort George, we find that, on Oct. 17th, 1780, Capt. Sherwood wrote to Colonel Henry Livingston, from on board the Carleton, "Major Chipman is also prisoner here with about forty men from Fort George."

There are various documents which show the measures taken to effect the liberation of their prisoners, but they are not of sufficient interest to quote here.

During the following winter both the English and the Americans appear to have been in a poor condition to resume hostilities. Though the former had withdrawn to the north, the latter had no heart to advance their lines, and had no force northward of Saratoga. The main line appears to have rested parallel to the Mohawk River. Thus the cold season passed in quiet, and the deserted ramparts of Fort George were left undisturbed.

Yet the people of the entire region lived in continual fear. Though the lakes were frozen, and the routes of travel were buried in snow, they knew that the spring would come upon them, unfettering the easily-navigated waters, and flinging wide all the gates. Therefore, on

January 23, 1781, Joseph McCracken, in behalf of the people of White Creek, addressed the Legislature of New York, saying that the march of Burgoyne left the region of Skenesboro' ruined, while the capture of Forts Ann and George, together with the ravages in Kingsbury and Queensbury, left the people to conclude that the British were bent upon their destruction. Moreover, the people had been kept "so long under arms" that they had been obliged to neglect their crops, and, unless immediate relief was given, they would withdraw altogether from that part of the country.

The Legislature, however, was poorly qualified to afford them any special aid, and if anything was done in response to this appeal, the record does not remain.

But, as the season advanced, the situation became invested with new complications, and the people of New York found that they might any day be obliged to contend with an enemy from Vermont, whose people had worked themselves up into a high state of excitement, in consequence of what they considered the aggressions of the government of Albany.

Moreover, the leaders of the people in Vermont were engaged in a system of double dealing; and, while representing themselves as friendly to the union of the States, and ardently desirous of an American victory, were, at the same time, carrying on secret negociations with the British. And whatever may have been the real designs of these men, it is clear that they managed all their negociations in such a way as to be ready to drop either party at any moment when it might serve their purpose.

It is true that they cordially hated both the British and the people of New York, and yet the more intense dislike appears to have been reserved for their foes of the common American household. Ethan Allen probably reflected the spirit of the leaders; and what he thought we may gather from a letter written by General Schuyler, at Saratoga, May 19, 1781. He says:

"Yesterday Major McCracken was with me and informed me that Ethan Allen had some days ago been at White Creek attempting to seduce the inhabitants from their allegiance to the State, that in conversation with him, he asked what part the Grants would take in case the enemy attempted to penetrate into the country. Allen replied that he would neither give nor take any assistance from New York." ("Clinton Papers," No. 3729.)

And, while this state of things continued, a transaction occurred which is of interest at this time, chiefly for the reason that it relates to the history of Fort George, the subject now under consideration.

We find that, on April 16th, Governor Clinton wrote to General Schuyler ("Clinton Papers," No. 3632) in regard to the secret negociations of the leaders in Vermont, and inclosed a letter on the subject from General Washington. In regard to Harris and Fish, who are mentioned therein, he says that he has "some reason to believe that they may both be confided in."

The letter of Washington, which does not appear in his published "Works," edited by Sparks, runs as follows, excepting one paragraph, which has no bearing upon the subject before us:

"HEAD QUARTERS, NEW WINDSOR 15. *April* 1781.
"DEAR SIR

"The bearer Mr Fish of Saratoga district came to me this morning, with the intelligence of which the inclosed is a copy. How he obtained it from one Harris, he will inform your Excellency. Harris, whose character perhaps your Excellency may be acquainted with, is to meet the party under Ensign Smith the 20th of this month—is to convey a packet to Albany and to carry another back to them. He proposed to Fish to seize him at a place to be agreed upon and to take the letters from him. But I think a better way would be to let him carry the letters and answers in the first instance to General Schuyler, who might contrive means of opening them without breaking the seal, take copies of the contents, and then let them go on. By this means we should become masters of the whole plot, whereas, were we to seize Harris upon his first tour, we should break up the chain of communication, which seems providentially so thrown into our hands. Should your Excellency approve the measures which I have suggested, you will be pleased to write to Genl Schuyler upon the subject, and desire him, should business call him from Albany, to leave the conduct of the affair in proper hands in his absence. I have promised Fish that both he and Harris shall be handsomely rewarded if they execute the business with fidelity.

*   *   *   *   *   *

"With the highest Respect and
"Esteem   I am
"Y^r Excellency
"Most o' Ser^t.
"G. WASHINGTON."

("Clinton Papers," No. 3633.)

The communication referred to is to the following effect:

"(Copy)   *March* 29. 81

"Being on the frontier in the neighborhood of Skenesborough on the 16th instant and being taken to be a tory were introduced to a party of the Enemy from Canada as commanded by Ensign Thos Smith late of Albany and David Higginbottom, Caleb Closen and Andrew Rukeley the whole four in number come on to a plot to destroy the independence of this and other States, it not being possible for me to betray them in safety concluded it best to act the hypocrite for once and succeeded so far as to draw from them that the grants had capitulated privately to lay down their arms on the approach of the British, which is to be done early this spring, when the British are to proceed to Fort George and take possession and fortify on Gages Hill,* for what purpose they now have their boats and shipping ready framed at St Johns and other places, to bring and put into Lake George with all other preparations, even their pickets to fortify the above post with. I further learned that their strength consists in eight thousand troops and Loyalists, and many in the State of New York were concerned, gentle & simple, not only on the frontier, but throughout

" From the M at Evening
"to the 22." ("Clinton Papers," No. 3633.)

What was the result of the foregoing transaction it is impossible to say. Possibly the men were well-meaning babblers, excited by the prospect of reward. As regards General Schuyler, however, he ultimately came to the conclusion that the leaders of Vermont, instead of plotting against the American cause, were engaged in the equally dangerous and dishonorable part of deceiving the authorities of Great Britain.† Nevertheless, he continued to watch the Vermonters, and, on May 4, 1781, he wrote to Governor Clinton that he intended to make a full examination of the subject.

---

* For a reference to this, *see* note on Fort Gage, at page 6. The author does not remember having seen any other allusion to " Gage's Hill " in the many contemporaneous manuscripts that he has examined. Beyond doubt, the hill referred to is that which afforded the site of the old fort, called " Fort Gage."

† The author here desires to express no opinion in regard to the real intentions of Vermont, as represented by her leaders. Nevertheless, the regret may be expressed that any should attempt to *justify* what they claim to be the precise intentions of those men. There is something that is worth more than immunity from temporary inconvenience, and which can never compensate for the loss of good faith between nations, as also between man and man.

CHAPTER VIII.

RITING to Governor Clinton, May 4, 1781, having his attention all the while closely given to the movements on the Grants, Gen. Schuyler says:

"That the enemy intend to take post more to the south than were [*sic*] they are at present, I really believe, but I cannot imagine that they mean permanently to do it on this side of Lake George;—should they fortify there at present it must evidently be with a design to take advantage of any movement of Sir Henry Clinton. A few days ago I advised General [James] Clinton that some of the British ships were arrived at Crown Point."

In the same letter he also says:

"The garrison here has been ten days without any meat, except what they procure by marauding, every eatable animal in this part of the country is already expended. Not a single scout can be kept out and I fear that Harris's last account will speedily be verified, and that a great majority of the troops here will go off to the enemy, (they may move leisurely to Fort George or Skenesborough and be there received into the enemies' boats) unless provision is instantly procured for them." ("Clinton Papers," No. 3691.)

At this time the condition of affairs on the frontiers of New York was truly deplorable. North of Saratoga, in the region of Lake George, the people were without defence, it being impossible to maintain a force at so distant a locality as Fort George.

In the meanwhile, the deplorable dissensions with Vermont grew apace, and frequent appeals were made to violence, so that troops were urgently needed for the protection of the citizens against the Green Mountain desperadoes. Happily, therefore, the British did not advance far on the lakes. Nevertheless, the summer air was thick with rumors, and the British were ever "coming." At last the imaginations of the inhabitants took on the form of the following communication from General Stark:

"Head Quarters
"half past 6 O c^k Saratoga
"11th *Octbr* 1781

"Dear Sir

"By Information this moment receid I am Informed that the Enemy are now in reality on this side of Lake George. for Gods sake hurry on with all the Force you can collect as perhaps this may be the Last Information I can give you until they are in reality here I can Give no Information of their Force but we must be prepared for the Worst.

"I am Dear Sir you
"very Hum^l Servt.
John Starke.

"B. Genl Gansevort." ("Clinton Papers," No. 4060.)

The next day, October 12, General Schuyler followed up Stark, in a letter to Governor Clinton, saying:

"This moment I received an express from Gen: Stark advising me that the Enemy had landed between Lake George & Saratoga." ("Clinton Papers," No. 4064.)

Governor Clinton immediately ordered General Rensaelear to be in readiness to march with his brigade; and, meanwhile, the alarm was spread abroad in print; for the "New York Journal," giving the Fishkill news of October 18, 1781, says:

"Accounts from the northward, give us strong indications of a hostile visit in that quarter. It is said that they have advanced to the South End of Lake George, in some force, but their numbers not ascertained ... Energetic measures are taking by the militia in that vicinity; a brigade of regular troops, part of which are already at Albany, passed through this town last Monday, on their way to Fish-Kill Landing, and there to embark on board of vessels to carry them up."

But the old cry of "Wolf!" did not, at least in this particular region, again meet its traditional reward; and, October 26th, General Heath wrote to Governor Clinton, from Continental Village, saying

"It is really surprising that accounts from the northward are so vague and uncertain—At one time the Enemy are beyond the lakes,— at another between them, and sometimes it is not known where they are." ("Clinton Papers," No. 4097.)

On the same day, October 26, the Assembly of New York, in an address to Governor Clinton, in which they said:

"It gives as great satisfaction to find that, notwithstanding the Extent of our frontier Settlements and the desultory War, carried on by a barbarous Enemy, fewer depredation have been committed than we had Reason to apprehend; Attributable, under God, to the Vigilance and activity of the Forces Stationed for their Protection, and with you, we confide that the regular Troops and Levies lately detached for their Defence, will be sufficient to repel the threatened Invasion of the Enemy.

"Permit us, Sir, to express the high Sense we entertain of your judicious Arrangements of our State Troops, and of the distinguished Exertions, which have on every Occasion, been made by your Excellency, to defend the Frontiers against the hostile attacks of our merciless Enemies." ("Journal of Assembly," 1781, p. 9.)

Yet their applause had hardly died away when the enemy actually appeared; and the "New York Packet," of November 1, reported truly that a party of British, under Major Ross, had come down Oneida Lake, burning dwellings and committing depredations, afterwards crossing the Mohawk River. Colonel Willett met them, however, and secured a decided victory.

November 3d, a second victory was reported as achieved by the same officer. From the "New Jersey Journal," of November 21, 1781, we learn that the commanding general at Poughkeepsie, issued an order recognizing the victory of Colonel Willett, and saying:

"The General has the pleasure of acquainting this army, that the enemy have been completely disappointed in their designs on the northern frontiers of this state, in consequence of the measures adopted to receive them in the vicinity of the Lakes * * * * That part of their force which was to proceed over the Lakes, has not dared to land on this side."*

In all these operations Fort George made no figure, as neither party found it advisable to throw forces forward to such an undesirable point; and, when winter came again, the position was hemmed in by the ice and snow.

With the return of spring (1782), the enemy, now disheartened by the reverses sustained in the South, made no effort to renew hostilities; and the people on the border of New York were quite as much in fear of the Vermonters as of anything. Yet, in the autumn, the alarm was sounded, and, in October, Jacob Bayley wrote to Governor Clinton, from Mowbury, as follows:

"Ten days ago I had intelligence which I depended upon from St. Johns that the enemy were moving in force up Lake Champlain that an Expedition [would go] Southward from that place, the Tenth of Oc-

---

* The full report of Willett may be seen in the "New Jersey Journal," November 28, 1781.

tober, also that a force was going by the way of Oswego *** The enemy will try to destroy Albany and Establish Vermont this season as well as to support Vermont in opposition to Congress *** I lay on my arms night and day being in Danger both from Britton and Vermont."

In a postscript, he adds:

"this minute I have Certain Inteligonce that the Enemy are Determined to Destroy Albany this fall that Vermont will make a great noies by calling in the militia &c but you may depend it will not be to oppose the Enemy but to Deceive the populous and prevent the militia from assisting you." ("N. Y. State Legislative Papers," MS.)

Thus, we have another illustration of the declaration of Ethan Allen, already quoted, that he would neither give nor take aid from New York.

Yet, notwithstanding all these threatening appearances, a peaceable solution of the Vermont difficulties was reached, while the return to friendly relations with the mother country extinguished the prospect of foreign invasion, and left Fort George in the wilderness, a forgotten relic of the past.

After its surrender by Captain Chipman, in 1780, it does not appear that Fort George was ever of any real practical use, or even that it possessed a garrison. Occasionally it may have furnished a refuge for raiders, and lodgings for the strolling scouts; but a position selected originally with so little judgment, and fortified with such limited strength, must of necessity find its level in the estimate of military. men, by whom it was ultimately abandoned as a post which it was not worth while to keep. In the War of 1812 it was not thought of.

But, though the military authorities lost all interest in the locality, civilians were fully alive in regard to the financial importance of the entire region. While of very moderate agricultural value, it possessed forests of no mean worth; and, besides, Lake St. Sacrament still possessed its advantages as a route of travel for passengers bound to Canada. Accordingly, many old soldiers who had served in the campaigns around the lake, and consequently had claims upon their country, remembered the sites of their former watch-fires, and petitioned for grants of land, as was also done by many of the survivors of the French war previous to the outbreak of the Revolution. When hostilities with England ceased, among other petitions laid before the authorities was the following:

"The Petition of Jonathan Pitcher, Gurdon Chamberlin, Wyatt Chamberlin and Isaac Doty residing on a Tract of Land at the South End of Lake George commonly called Garrison-Land, humbly sheweth; That Your Petitioners, some time since, being desirous to emigrate from the Old Settlements and to fix ourselves on the Frontier of the State, did obtain, from the Surveyor Genl of the State, Leases of the Lands whereon we now reside, which Leases being only for the Term of One Year induceth us to address Your Hon'ble Body on the Sub-

ject—Your Petitioners having removed our families to this place at great Expence from a very considerable distance, ardently wish to continue on the same, and do, most humbly pray that our Leases may be renewed for as long a Term of time as your Hon'ble Body shall deem most eligible; or that any other mode may be adopted whereby your petitioners may be allowed to occupy the premises.
"LAKE GEORGE *Dec.* 30 1783."

("New York Legislative Papers," MS.)

December 19, 1784, Jacobus Van Schoonhoven and Gerardus Clute, of Half Moon, say in their petition to the Legislature:

"That your Petitioners are desirous of accepting a Lease from the State of the Landing Place at Fort George and fifty acres of meadow land adjoining the Same—as also the Exclusive right of Ferriage from said landing to Ticonderoga—also the sole Exclusive privilege of Keeping a Tavern at the Same Landing insomuch that no other person is to be permitted to keep a tavern within the distance of half a mile from Said Landing. That your petitioners propose and are willing to enter into a Covenant for erecting a House & Barn and a sufficient number of Ferry Boats for the purpose aforesaid."*

February following, William Cobb and Lyman Hitchcock made a similar request, though apparently with poor results. Eventually the greater portion of the land in this vicinity was granted to James Caldwell, and the town which sprang up at the end of Lake George took the proprietor's name, which it still bears.

In course of time the shores of this beautiful lake possessed quite a numerous population; and the number of the inhabitants is now slowly increasing year by year, many of whom are attracted by the romantic recollections of the place, and the rare beauty of the scenery, which, whatever may be the changes that are to come, can never lose its ineffable charm.

But the student of History may always enjoy a twofold pleasure in visiting and lingering around the site of Old Fort George. The flippant tourist who visits the lake as an act of fashionable propriety

---

* Connected with the petition of those wanting lands and other emoluments, is one bearing date of January 4, 1784, from Lieut.-Colonel Robert Cochran, of "the Second New York Regiment of foot in the Service of the United States," who "Humbly sheweth" to the "people of the State of New York in Senate and Assembly convened,"

"That very shortly after the commencement of Hostilities by the British Troops, your Petitioner at the head of a small party of Volunteers, and at the evident Risk and Hazard of his Life attacked and carried with the British Garrisons at Crown Point and Ticonderoga, by which fortunate and unexpected Event a very considerable quantity of heavy artillery and military stores were secured for the use of the United States, as many of the members of this Honorable House now present can attest." ("N. York Legislative Papers," MS.)

This statement is, of course, about as trustworthy as that by Ethan Allen, who likewise professed that he was "at the head" of this same "small party," and who claimed the exclusive glory of the capture of Ticonderoga.

will, indeed, hardly appreciate the feelings of the intelligent antiquary who seeks to make himself familiar with each storied site. The forces engaged around the lake were trivial compared with the armies that have since done battle to maintain the Independence which was in northern New York, at the outset, so largely achieved. Then, as regards Fort George itself, we might have dismissed the subject with a few words, saying that there never *was* any Fort George, since the structure that bore the name was simply the bastion of an *intended* fortification. But here the interest does not depend upon numbers and architecture. In a historical point of view, the strength of an army is of little more concern than the stature of its commander. It is the *morale* of the struggle that chiefly excites reflection. At least the antiquary finds it so at Fort George, where he hears no story of numbers, and is not impressed, as is some times the case at Ticonderoga, by the extent of the military remains. Only one insignificant ruin is now found on the old grounds at the head of the lake for which kings contended through many long years. So obscure is the site, that those who go rapidly over the route often do not see it at all; while others confound the ruins of Fort George with the remains of an ancient limekiln that lie, an almost undistinguishable heap, near by. But the site is, nevertheless, readily discovered, and, in approaching the lake from Glen's Falls, it will be found on the right of the ancient military road, embowered among the hemlocks and pines. The sally-port is gone, and the rudely-built walls are crumbling to their fall. Plants and creepers in many places hold together the loose stones laid by tired hands that long since found rest. Within the inclosure, sheep browse among the mullein stalks, and the tinkling of the cow-bell floats out from among the trees, falling musically upon the ear. It is a quiet place, indeed. Fort George has known its last alarm, and fired its last gun. On a mild summer day, everything is bathed in the atmosphere of peace, which is only intensified by the glimpse of the sleeping Lake St. Sacrament, which, from the ramparts, may be seen through the sun-smitten haze. Here the antiquary may generally meditate undisturbed; though occasionally the silence will be invaded by some solitary visitor like himself, or by some noisy troop of young tourists from the hotel, who rush suddenly from out the wood, and, with shut sun-shades and umbrellas, charge, in mimic war, and with a merry shout, upon the defenseless walls of Fort George. But, anon, the enemy retreats, when he is left again to dwell at leisure upon his historical notes, to identify the localities, and recall the great memories of ambitious England, in connection with the struggles of proud but dreaming France. Yet, as regards the dreams of France, they were not altogether baseless. While, in the nature of things, it was hardly possible, under ordinary circumstances, for descendants of the effete Latin race to become the rulers of the New World, yet, at one time, French ambition seemed almost on the point of realization. And it is, therefore, worth while here to remember the fact, that, in connection with Fort George, the movement was begun which was destined to end in the complete demolition of the French power in America. And more; the founding of Fort George was the *initiatory act* in Amherst's campaign, during which the tide of French prosperity turned, and the French themselves were driven from the beautiful lake to which they originally gave the name. When Montressor laid out the plan of the work, he in reality inaugurated the Anglo-American success that led the way for the establishment of the Great Republic. Therefore, however little we may owe to the strength of the structure itself, its connection with American Independence is every way deeply interesting. This circumstance alone will justify the antiquary in the bestowal of much study upon the history of these venerable ruins, which at no distant period are destined to pass entirely away.

APPENDIX.

I.

ORDERLY BOOK OF JAMES McGEE,

AT FORT GEORGE, JULY AND AUGUST, 1776.

[COPY FROM THE ORIGINAL MS. IN THE NEW YORK STATE LIBRARY, 1871.]

FORT GEORGE *July* 17th 1776

Rigmental orders

PAROLE SCHYLAR

Gaurds to Be Mount^d As Usial officers for tomorow Capⁿ Martin By order of the Comanding officer   PETTER B. TIARS *Adujant*

Rigmental orders Fort George July the 16th 1776

PAROLE WASHINGTON

All officers and Soldiers are forbid to go Among the Small pox and By no maner Enoculate or Sufer them Selves to Be Enoculated on pain to be punished^d Without the Benifit of A Court Martial Guards to Be Mount^d as Usial Officers for tomorow Capⁿ Wright By order of the Comanding officer   PETTER B TIARS *Adujant*

Rigmental orders Fort George July 18th 1776

PAROLE

A Rigmental Court Martial to Sett Emediately to try Such prisoners as may Be Brought Before them. Gaurd to Be Mount^d as Usial officers for tomorow Capⁿ Van ranselar By order of Co^l Ten Eyck
      PETTER B TIARS *Adujant*

Rigmental order Fort George July the 19 1776

PAROLE ECOPUS

The Rigmental Court Martial to Be contin^d to try Such Prisoners as may Be Brought Before them Gaurd to Be Mount^d as Usial officers for tomorow Capⁿ Edmerson By order of Col Ten Eyck
      PETTER B. TEARS *Adujant*

APPENDIX TO

Communications threatened, 31; Recruits for, 32; Surgeon for, 32, at, 33, Garrison, 33; By Burgoyne's approach, 35; Garrison in danger, 36; its condition described, 36; Stores removed from, 37; Schuyler marches for, 37; the fort destroyed, 37; Garrison escapes, 38; Called "Fort Edward," 39; Col. Anstruther at, 39; Wyncoop's seat at, 40; Soldier, ill. Captured by Arnold, 41; General Irvine commands at, 41; Secret orders concerning, 41; Stores carried from, 41; one Cannon Eye coast clear, 45; Burgoyne on the Fort George route, 46; Gansevoort commands at, 49; Surrendered by Chipman, 49; his vindication, 49; an "intended" attack, 50; Terms of surrender, 51; Prisoners taken, 52; Reports concerning, 54; Number held, 54; Result of invasion, 55; enemy to take possession of Fort George, 56; approach of enemy to, 59; its importance lost, 61; not used in war, 61; Petitions for land around, 61; Tavern at, 62; Ferry at, 62; the ruins of, 65; Garrison at, 65; kept at, 65; Garrison land petitioned for, 61; Gates (Gen.), 40; Gage's Hill, 57; Gansevoort (Col. Peter), 53, 65; Green Mountain Boys, abolish the law, 29; Graydon, 22; Haldimand, 38; may Be Brought Before the enemy, Killed, Haldiman (Edward), 23; Haldiman (Gov.), 23; Herrick (Samuel), Letter to Gen. Powell, 31; Hinman, 1, 2, 9; Horton, 42; Indians (Disturbances with), 9; Island in the fort, 43; Jessup (Major), 53; Jersey Blues scalped, 7; Johnson (Gen. W.), knighted, 2; Fails to improve his advantage, 3; Johnson (Sir W.), 2; Jogues (Rev. I.), 2; Kay, 3; Ketcham (Stephen), Information of, 30; Knox (his Journal), 4; Lake George (Route over), 1; Battle of, 2; Men at, 9; Ferry at, 9, 40, 3 privates to be Discharged; Lake St. Sacrament, 1; Lincoln (Benj.), Letter to, 58; Litle Boards and to Suffer none to be taken away by the carpenters with Livingston (Col.), 28; Loudon (Earl of), 3; Martial officers for tomorow Capn Wright, 55; McCracken (Joseph), 55; McKesson (John), 24; McLew (Major), 28; McCrickin Moses Creek, 25; Mead (lt.), 3; McGinkin (—), 29; Mercer (—), 28; Minult (Samuel), Letter to Clinton, 29; Montgomery (Gen.), 4; Mott (Capt. Ed.), Disperses rioters, 20, 45; Montcalm Captures Fort William Henry, 3, 53; Munroe (Col.), 3; Montressor (Capt.), Plans Fort George, 4; Mount Independence, 11; surrenders, 11; Norberg (John), his petition, 11; New Jersey officers for tomorow Capn Martin by order of Colonel Ten Eyck Parks (Elijah), 14; Parks (Ephraim), 14; Palmer (Gen.), 42; Philadelphia Barras (Noah), 14; Potts (Noah), 10; Privates (Ld. Stair), officers for tomorow Capn Rex of Colonel Ten Eyck Rensaelear (Gen.), 59; Regiments, 28; Commanders of, 20, 38; Reed (Gen.), 39; Riedesel (The Baroness), 39; Journal of, 39; Rogers, Albany, 60; Rogers (Bernard), Takes Fort George, 11; Note on, 11; Goes to Albany, 14; Strasslar expresses, Rocque (Mary Ann), Plan of Fort George, 5; Rigaud attacks Fort William Henry, 3; Sabath Day Point, 70, 73; Shirley (Gen. William), 3; Such prisoners as may Be Killed, 33; St. Clair (Gen.), "a great soldier," 35; his retreat, 36; Rensselaer's Compy of Col. Schaick (Cpt.), 31, 32; Schuyler to Washington, 22; Snyder (John), his Memorial, 18; Ticonderoga, 2; Winter expedition against, 3; Amherst attacks Ticonderoga, 8; Delays at, 8, 18; in ruins, 18; Reinforced, 20; Plan of, 19; Tryon (Gov.), 13; Tiars (Adjutant Peter B.), 65; Tryon (Gov.), 13; Trumbull (John), 24; Livingston (Jonathan), 16; Vermont, her negotiations with the British, her hostilities, 17; Washington (Gen.), Letter on, 58; Woedtke (Baron of), 26; Warren, 10, his Mount, 10; Wright, 55; Wilkinson (Sickness of), 26; Letter to Gates, 34; Williams, Dr Tyres, Letter, 8, 9.

FINIS.

Rig^(mt) orders fort George July 27^(th) 1776

A Rigmental Court Martial to Be Set to morow Morning to try Such prisoners as may Be Brought Before them Gaurds to Be Mount^d to Morow As Usial officer for tomorow Cap^n Edmenton

PETTER GANSEVOORT
Lt Coll

Rigm^t Orders Fort George July the 28^(th) 1776

PAROLE GADSON

Gaurds to Be Mount^d as Usial officer for to morow Cap^n V^n Ranselar   PETTER GANSEVOORT Lt Col

Rig^t Orders July the 29th, 1776

PAROLE LIBERTY

Gaurds to be Moun^d as Usial officer for tomorow Cap^n V^n Nasa

PETTER GANSEVOORT Lt Col^l

Garison Orders fort George 30 July 1776

PAROLE SUCCESS

Every Oficer Station^d At this Garison is order^d to Aply to the Adujant of Col^l V^n Shaccks Regm^t for General Schuylers Orders of the 24th of May Last And As far as it relates to Ether of them they will Comply With Said orders if Any officer After this Should Be found Neglijent of Complying With Said order I Shall Be O Blige^d to take Such Steps As Will Be Very Disagreeabel to Both them and Me the officers Not on Duty Are Likewise order^d to Attend the Parade At the Beating of the Troop and the retreat they are likewise order^d to turn out to Exercise Every Afternoon At 4 oclock With the More Gaurds to Be Mount^d tomorow As Usial officers for tomorow Cap^n Mercelis

PETTER GANSEVOORT Lt Col^l

Rigment^l orders Fort George July 31^(st) 1776

PAROLE SHUYLAR

A corporal and Six privates to fitch A Batteau Load of fire Wood for the use of the Generals family Gaurds to be Mount^d as Usial officer for tomorow Cap^n Wright   PETTER GANSEVOORT Lt Col

Garison orders August the 1^(th) 1776

PAROLE SANDY

the Court of Enquirery Sat this Day is order^d to Sett tomorow Gaurds to be Mount^d tomorow as Usial officers for tomorow Cap^n Martin

PETTER GANSEVOORT Lt Col

Garison orders Fort George August the 2^(th) 1776

PAROLE McDOUGAL

A Garison Court Martial to Set tomorow morning at Nine O'clock to try Such Prisoners as may be Brout Before them Gaurds to Be Mount^d as Usial officer for tomorow Cap^n V^n Renselar

PETTER GANSEVOORT
Lt Col

Garison orders Fort George Augus the 3^d 1776

PAROLE INDUSTRY

Gaurds to be Mount^d As usial officer for tomorow Cap^n Merceles

PETTER GANSEVOORT
Lt Col

Garison Orders Fort George August the 4th 1776.

PAROLE GRANT

Gaurds to Be Mount^d as Usial Officer for tomorow Cap^n Martin

PETTER GANSEVOORT
Lt Col^o

Garison orders Fort George August 5th 1776

PAROLE COOTS

Gaurds to Be Mount^d as Usial officer for tomorow Cap^n Edmuston

PETTER GANSEVOORT Lt Col^o

Garison Orders Fort George August the 6th

PAROLE LEWIS

A Garison Court Martial to Be Sett at Eight Oclock tomorow Morning to try Such prisoners As may Be Brought Before them Gaurds to Be Mount^d as Usial officer for tomorow Cap^n V^n Nasy

PETTER GANSEVOORT Lt Col^o

Garison Orders Fort George August the 7th 1776

PAROLE McDOUGAL

Gaurd to Be Mount^d as Usial Officer for tomorow Cap^n Merceles the Court Martial Sat yesterday is to Continue Seting to Day

PETTER GANSEVOORT Lt Col^o

Garison Orders Fort George August 8th 1776

PAROLE SCHUYLAR

Gaurds to Be Mount^d as Usial officer for to morow Cap^n V^n Ranselar

PETTER GANSEVOORT Lt Col^o

Garison Orders Fort George August the 9th 1776

PAROLE FROMAN

three privates to Be Detach^d from the Main Gaurd to the Corporals Gaurd Which is Kept at the General Hospital from Which Place they Are to furnish one at the point formerly Call^d fort Wilam henry Gaurds to Be Mount^d as Usial Officer for tomorow Cap^n Edmeston

PETTER GANSEVOORT Lt Col^o

Garison orders Fort George August the 10th

Gaurds to Be Mount^d as Usial officer for tomorow Cap^n V^n Neys
PETTER GANSEVOORT Lt Col^o

PAROLE TILTON

Garison orders parole Ten Eyck August 11th 1776

A Garison Court Martial to Set tomorow Morning to try Such prisoners as shall Be Brought Before them Gaurds to Be Mount^d as Usial officers for to morow Cap^n Merceles
PETTER GANESVOORT Lt Col

Garison Orders Fort George August the 12th 1776

PAROLE ANDERSON

Gaurds to Be Mount^d as Usial officer for tomorow Cap^n V^n Ranselar
PETTER GANSEVOORT Lt Col

Garison orders Fort George August the 13th 1776

PAROLE RANSELAR

Gaurds to Be Mount^d as Usial officer for tomorow Cap^n Edmeston
PETTER GANSEVOORT Lt Col^o

Garison orders Fort George August the 14th 1776

PAROLE LISBON

one Serg^t and 15 privates to go over the Lake tomorow Morning Gaurd to Be Mount^d to morow as Usial officer for to morow Cap^n V^n Neys
PETTER GANSEVOORT Lt Col

Garison orders Fort George August 15th

PAROLE V^N SHAICK

A Garison Court Martial to Sett tomorow Morning to try such prisoners as shall Be Brought Before them Gaurds to Be Mount^d as Usial officer for to morow Cap^n Martin
PETTER GANSEVOORT Lt Col

Garison Orders Fort George August 16th

PAROLE

Gaurds to Be Mount^d tomorow as Usial officer for tomorow Cap^n V^n Ranselar
PETTER GANSEVOORT Lt Col^o

Garison orders Fort George August 17th 1776

PAROLE PHILADELPHIA

one Serg^t and 15 Privates to Embark to morow Morning in three Batries to cary Provision over Lake George Gaurds to Be Mount^d as Usial officer for tomorow Cap^n Edmeston
PETTER GANSEVOORT Lt Col

Garrison orders—the First Capts. of rapids, and takes out. The danger she 'scaped on those fresh water
For twice she crossed Lakes George and   seas,*
Champlain;   And from the salt Western Ocean,
Lake Ontario, Lake Erie, and Lake Huron, I'll sing when my head is some night more at
Saint Peter's, Saint Francis, and Lake Saint   tomorow Capn Martin
Clair, thrice;   I'l intrude now too much might my readers
Garison orders—Parole Victory Fort George Augt 19 displease,—
Which made no short female campaign. My limbs, too, require locomotion.

Gaurds to Be Mounted as Usial officer for to morow Capn Vn Ran-
selar   Petter Gansevoort
(From Miscellanies by an Officer [Arent Schuyler De Peyster], Vol. I. pp. 50, 58.)   Lt Coll°
Dumfries, 1813.

II.

DE PEYSTER'S TOUR TO QUEBEC.

The days that have left no history are sometimes illustrated by old ballads. In connection with the early history of Fort George, we may therefore give some lines, of a slightly humorous character, from a now scarce volume of "Miscellanies by an Officer," printed at Dumfries, Scotland, in 1813. The author of the volume was Colonel Arent Schuyler de Peyster, an officer of the British army, who appears to have crossed Lake George twice before the outbreak of the American Revolution. The date of the passage across the lake described in the accompanying lines cannot, perhaps, be determined, though it appears to have taken place while the forces occupied Fort George to fire an evening gun, since it is not likely that they could have heard the gun from Ticonderoga.

The narrative is very eliptical, but, while the story lacks unity, we have some glimpses of the condition of things not otherwise afforded. The allusion to Vaudrueil is, of course, incorrect, as he had nothing to do with the massacres of Bloody Pond.

At the time Colonel de Peyster crossed the lake, there appears to have been no place of entertainment of any sort at the head of the lake, as they encamped for the night. At this time the Indians were prowling about, and the batteau-men, as they worked their way along, were accustomed to sing snatches of French songs.

The wolves appear to have been in full force, and the grim humor implied in the collection of bones by "Susan," is very likely founded in fact. Sabbath-Day Point was the scene of many a bloody transaction, and, at that period, abounded in such souvenirs. It is not at all wonderful that, amid such scenes, "She" should start in afright at every unfamilar sound.

But we must make a few remarks in regard to the author of the lines in question. Valentine's "New York Manual," page 571, says, that

Colonel Arent Schuyler de Peyster, son of Colonel de Heer Abraham de Peyster, was born in New York, June 27, 1736, and died at Dumfries, Scotland, at the advanced age of about eighty-seven. It is said that he was not only "a soldier and diplomatist, for he wielded a vigorous pen, and even shone in poetry, sufficiently so to merit a poetic notice from the celebrated Burns, with whom he broke a lance in verse."

One of Burns' fugitive pieces was addressed to him, beginning:

> "My honor'd Colonel, deep I feel
> Your int'rest in the poet's weal;
> Ah! how sma' head ha'e I to speel
>   The steep Parnassus
> Surrounded thus by bolus pill
>   And potion glasses."

Colonel de Peyster commanded at Michilimackinac, in the North-west, from 1774 till 1779. Probably he crossed Lake George on the way to his department, in 1774; but it was clearly a visit prior to that which he now describes.

Of the merit of his composition the reader will probably judge; and we need only observe here that, if with Burns he "broke a lance in verse," then, "in verse," he has also cruelly "cracked the legs of Time," to say the least. But we give the composition now, with the author's notes.

APPENDIX TO

From Saratoga to the River St. Lawrence,

ON HER WAY TO QUEBEC.

The wise and active conquer difficulties,
By daring to attempt, sloth and folly
Shiver and shrink at sight of toil and hazard,
And make the impossibility they fear.—ROWE.

SHE left Saratoga, at dawn of the day,
   And passed bloody pond without fear,*
   (Where the troops of Vaudreul, with dread Indian allies,
Scalped hundreds of Britons, ta'en there by surprise),
   And dropt, as she passed it, a tear.

Encamped at Lake George, as the sun disappeared,
   The bull-frogs in thorough bass croaking,
Soon brought on a tenor from perched whip-her-will,†
The screams of the wood-frogs,‡ in trebles so shrill,
   And buzz of muskettoes provoking.

On a wind-fallen tree, where I sat by her side,
   To guard my best treasure from harm,
She heard the screech owl, from an old blasted oak,
Set up a dead cry, at the wood-pecker's stroke,
   Which caused in her some small alarm.

The elk's whistling pipe, too, distinctly she heard;
And what every traveller's blood chills,—
The war-whoop of Indians, returning from war!
While the lone evening gun, discharged from afar,
   Re-echoed twelve times from the hills.

When all else was still, at the dead of the night,
   A boat, in the moon's wake, she spied;
In time went the oars, to the strokes-man's boat-song,
When all joined in chorus, and pulled all so strong,
   She swift through the water did glide.

   " Papillon vol, il vol,
     Papillon vol, sur L'aviron."§
Chorus—" Hotirre galere au fond,
     Ho tiere galere."‖

They landed, and dragged their batteau up the beach;
A fire was soon made for the pot;
Each stuck up a forked stick, with bear's meat to roast,
And then pitched their tents on the musical coast,
   As if to sojourn on the spot.

---

* The Indians who surprised the British, being in Canada.
† Called quack-qua-rie by the Indians.
‡ Their noise almost deafens.
§ There are two lines of a song set by the strokesman of the boat, to which every rower in turn composes as much.
‖ A chorus the Canadian boatmen attach to most of their aquatic songs.

The guide stove a keg, ready placed on its end,
  Before he sat down on his pack,
To take up his calumet; when, in a trice
  The commis cut every batteau-man a slice
From a roll of his bourgeois* tabac.

To them came the warriors, twelve in a canoe,
  Who eyed her ascaunt for a while,
And but for the war-pole,† 'twas pleasing to view
How they laughed, danced, and sung, as familar they grew,
  O'er a cup of dashed yankey‡ in style.

The war-chief invited my help-mate to dance,
  To which she so kindly complied,
And stept so in time to their hollow-tree drum,
The chief drank her health in a bumper of rum,
  While she by the fierce band was eyed.

This joyous scene changed to a dread thunder-storm,
  The rocks, woods, and waves, seemed on fire;
The warriors appalled, did like aspen-leaves shake,
Whose war-chief, alone, could stand near the bright lake,
  An emblem of Milton's hell sire.§

Encamped the next morning, at Sabbath-day Point,
  Miss *Susan* was quickly embowered,
While her mistress sat musing upon the moss stones;
Sue brought her check apron, crammed full of dried bones,
  Of a man, whom the wolves had devoured.

Still not disappointed, her kettle she boiled,
  At the boatmen's already-made fire,
And put in the tea, when the water was hot,
As all travellers do, when they've fractured the pot,
  Who do such refreshment require.

While salt pork was boiling, to give the men heart,
  And beds were preparing of heather,
The wolves a most hideous loud barking did make,
In chace of a buck, which soon took to the lake,
  Where heedless all plunged in together.

He crossed, but the pack, with their brushes all wet,
  Ran shaking them, when we all fired;
Thus peppered with buck-shot, they dared not to stop,
Where they might have had each a salted pork chop,
  Or man's flesh, by wolves more admired.

She next passed the block-house for Tycan-darougue,
  From whence the last evening-gun fired,
And heard one from Crown-point, just at setting sun,
But as a good day's work the boatmen had done,
  They halted that night, being tired.

From Crown-point a sloop crossed Champlain the next night,
  And towed the batteau by a line;
Becalmed for a while, we held fast by the trees,
Where gnats and wild sand-flies poor travellers do teaze,
  Or I could have wished the land mine.

Soon gad-flies and bad flies, of every kind,
  Drew blood, as Saint John's we approached;
Muskettoe nets there were of little avail,
For some would have pierced through a hogshead with ale,
  If ale had been blood to have broached.

The rapids, alarming, were shot to Shamblee;—
  " Push her off!—Hold her to!—Let her go!" ‖
The lady undaunted, still held up her head,
While *Susan* lay down on her *face*, almost dead,
  And falling, drew with her a beau.¶

---

* The bourgeois or merchant sends out his *commis*, or clerk, with charge of his goods up the Indian country.

† Bearing the scalps and dangling thereon.

‡ New England rum, much dashed with water.

§ As Satan is depicted standing, in the frontispiece of an old edition of " Paradise Lost."

‖ It being so difficult, from the impetuosity of the current, to keep the boat from over-setting.

¶ A gentleman who was little calculated for such a journey.

Thus ends the first canto of rapids and lakes,
    For twice she crossed Lakes George and Champlain;
Lake Ontario, Lake Erie, and Lake Huron, twice;
Saint Peter's, Saint Francis, and Lake Saint Clair, thrice;
    Which made no short female's campaign.

The danger she 'scaped on those fresh water seas,*
    And from the salt Western Ocean,
I'll sing when my head is some night more at ease,
T' intrude now too much might my readers displease,—
    My limbs, too, require locomotion.

---

* The waves run as high in these lakes as they do in the Atlantic

(From Miscellanies by an Officer [Arent Schuyler De Peyster], Vol. I., pp. 50-58.)

DUMFRIES, 1813.

MAP OF LAKE GEORGE.

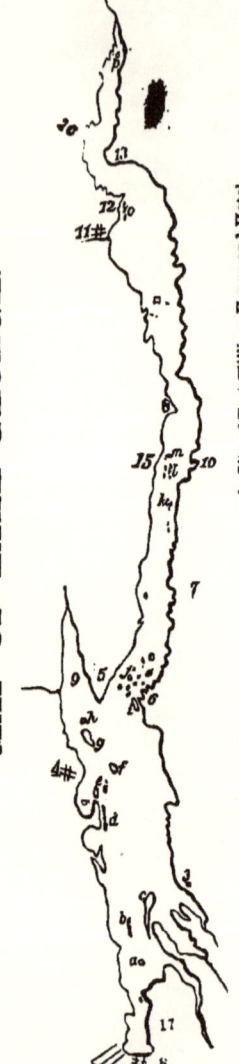

a. Diamond Island.
b. The Three Sisters.
c. Long Island.
d. The Three Brothers.
e. Recluse Island.
f. Dome Island.
g. Green Island.
h. Hog Island.
i. Fourteen-Mile Island.
j. The Narrows.
k. Floating Battery Islands.
l. Vicar's Island.
m. Harbor Island.
n. Odell's Island.
o. Friends' Islands.
p. Mutton, or Prisoner's Island.
q. Clay Island.

1. Site of Fort William Henry and Hotel.
2. Trout Pavilion.
4. Bolton.
5. Tongue Mountain.
6. Shelving Rock.
7. Black Mountain.
8. Sabbath Day Point.
9. North West, or Ganasouke Bay.
10. Bosom Bay.
11. Hague.
12. Friends' Point.
13. Anthony's Nose.
14. Ticonderoga.
15. Buck Mountain.
16. Rogers' Slide.
17. Peak of French Mountain.
18. Fort George.
≡≡≡ Montcalm's Intrenchments, 1757

Length of Lake...........................about 34 Miles.
Greatest Width............................ 4 "
Greatest Depth (Survey of 1755, 96 ft.) probably......200 feet.
Elevation above the Sea.........................340 "

INDEX.

ABERCROMBIE Attacks Ticonderoga, 3, 4.
Allen (Heman), 15, 44.
Allen (Ethan), a price put on his head, 9; captures Ticonderoga, 10; Letter of, 17; Resigns, 19; "More to be Dreaded than Death," 21; Intriguing, 55.
Artillery sent to Cambridge, 17.
Anstruther (Col.), 39, 40.
Amherst (General Jeffries), moves to Lake George, 4.
Artillery dug up, 6.
Arnold (Benedict), 14, 18, 46.
Beardsley (Reminiscences of), 9
Bailey (Jacob), 60.
Balcarras (Earl of), 46.
Boynton, History of West Point quoted, 12.
Barracks, 25.
Baldwin, 30.
Ballstown, 54.
Bennington mob, 21.
Boucherville, 40.
Burns (Robert), 71.
Burgoyne (Secret Orders of), 35, 41; Surrenders, 43.
Bourdon (Jean), 2.
Buell (Lieut.-Col.), 25.
Blind Rock, 22.
Bloody Pond (Fight at), 2, 23, 48, 51, 70.
Brown (Capt. John), 10; Attack on Ticonderoga, 42; at Diamond Isle, 42.
Cannon removed from Ticonderoga, 15.
Carroll (Charles), 21.
Carlton (Major), attacks the Americans, 47, 50.
Carnes (Major), 29.
Carroll (Bishop), 21.
Capitulation (Articles of), 52.
Campbell (Major), 7.
Caswell (Peter), 13.
Chamberlin (Wyat), 61.
Champlain, 73.
Chase (Mr.), 21.
Chipman (Capt. John), Commands at Fort George, 47; his Orders, 47, 48; Clinton's Aspersions of, 49; his Letter to the Press, 50; a Prisoner, 54.
Clinton (Gov.), 21, 47, 49, 51, 58, 62.
Connecticut Gazette, 52.
Cobb (Captain), 32.

Conspiracy of Vermont and the British, 56.
Continental Congress, 15.
Cochran (Col. Robert), his Petition, 62.
Court Martial, 47, 65.
Cobb (William), 62.
Crown Point, 1, 2, 73.
Craig (Capt.), 27.
Curtenius (Peter T.), 9.
Dally (Mr.), 20.
De Lancey (Proclamation of), 8.
Delaplace (Captain William), 10.
Defendorf (Henry), 32.
Deal (Sam.), 9.
Deane (Barnabas), Letter of, 18.
De Peyster (Col. Arent Schuyler), 70.
Diamond Island, Stories of, 41; Attack on, 43; Captain Aubrey Commands at, 43.
Dieskau (General), 2, 22.
Dartmouth (Earl of), 13.
Doty (Isaac), 61.
Dyck (C—— V.), 33.
Evans (Lewis), Essays, quoted, 1.
Element Hill, 5, 7.
Eyck (Col. Ten), 65.
Ferry at Fort George, 62.
Five Mile Run, 37.
Fort Edward, 8, 23, 34, 40.
Fort Gage, 6, 57.
Fort Ann Abandoned, 37.
Fort Stanwix, 4.
Fort Lyman, 2.
Fort William Henry (Building of), 3.
Franklin (Benjamin), 21.
Fort George Planned, 4; Situation of, 5; Rocque's plan of, 5; Workmen at, 8; Work ends, 8; Seized by Romans, 10; False reports of, 11; Surrendered by Nordberg, 12; Capture of, 14; Cannon removed to, 15, 17, 19; called "William Henry," 17, Boats Built at, 17; the command at, 19; Examined by Engineers, 19; Troops needed, 20; Carpenters sent to, 20; Activity at, 21; General Thomas leaves, 21; Condition of, 22; Schuyler at, 22; Graydon at, 22; Batteau at, 23; Exposed to enemy, 23; Gansevoort commander at, 24; Sickness at, 25; Barracks at, 25; Woedtke dies at, 26; Wilkinson sick at, 26, 27; Alarm at, 29; Dayton's regiment ordered to, 29; Hides wasted, 29

Communications threatened, 31; Flour at, 31; Recruits for, 32; Surgeon for, 32; Quiet at, 33; Hospital at, 33; Capt. McCrackin commands at, 34; Burgoyne's approach, 35; Garrison in danger, 36; its condition described, 36; Stores removed from, 37; Schuyler marches for, 37; the fort destroyed, 37; Garrison escapes, 38; Called "Fort Edward," 39; Col. Anstruther at, 39; Wyncoup's fleet at, 39; "Rebels" at, 39; Riedesel maintains communication of, 41; Lieut. Irwine commands at, 41; Secret orders concerning, 41; stores carried from, 41; Prisoners taken near, 43; the coast clear, 45; Burgoyne on the Fort George route, 46; Garrison orders, 47, 48; Capt. Chipman commands at, 49; Surrendered by Chipman, 49; his vindication, 49; an "intended fort," 50; Terms of surrender, 51; Prisoners taken, 52; Reports concerning, 54; Fort George deserted, 54; Result of invasion, 55; Plans of enemy to take possession of Fort George, 56; Rumored approach of enemy to, 39; its importance lost, 61; not used in war of 1812, 61; Petitions for land around, 61; Tavern at, 62; Ferry at, 62; the ruins of, 63; Reflections on, 63; Orderly Book kept at, 65.
Garrison Orders, 47, 48, 65.
Garrison land petitioned for, 61.
Gates (General Thos.), 23, 24, 43.
Gage's Hill, 57.
Gansevoort (Col. Peter), 53, 65.
Green Mountain Boys, abolish the law, 20.
Graydon, 22, 23.
Half Moon, 20.
Hamilton (Gen.), 40.
Haldiman (Gov.), 53.
Herrick (Samuel), Letter to Gen. Powell, 43.
Hinman (Col.), 19.
Horicon, 3.
Indians (Disturbances with), 9.
Islands possessed by the French, 7; Fight at, 7.
Jessop (Major), 53.
Jersey Blues scalped, 7.
Johnson (Gen. W.), knighted, 2; Fails to improve his advantages, 3; Governor of Guernsey, 4, 22.
Jogues (Rev. I.), 2.
Kayaderosseras (Patent of), 13.
Ketchem (Stephen), Information of, 30.
Knox (his Journal), 4.
Lake George (Route over), 1; Battle of, 2; Men at, 9; Ferry at, 9, 40, 71, 72.
Lake St. Sacrament, 1; Name of, 2, 61.
Lincoln (Gen.), 41, Letter to Yates, 42.
Livingston (Col.), 50.
Loudon (Earl of), 3.
Malcolm (Col.), 50.
McCracken (Joseph), 55.

McKesson (John), 24.
McCrea (Miss), Death of, 36.
Moses Creek, 35.
Minott (Samuel), Letter to Clinton, 21.
Montgomery (Gen.), 21.
Mott (Capt. Ed.), Disperses rioters, 20, 45.
Montcalm captures Fort William Henry, 3, 53.
Munroe (Col.), 3.
Montressor (Col.), Plans Fort George, 4.
Mount Independence, 33, 43.
Nordberg (John), his petition, 11; Surrenders Fort George, 12; Dismissed, 14.
Parks (Daniel), "Took the key," 13; his tablet, 13.
Parks (Elijah), 14.
Parks (Ephraim), 14.
Palmer (Gen.), 42.
Phelps (Noah), 10.
Potts (Noah), 10.
Potts (Dr.), 26; Letters to Gates, 27, 33, 35.
Recluse Island, 4.
Rensaelear (Gen.), 59.
Regiments, 28; Commanders of, 28, 31.
Riedesel (Gen.), 39.
Riedesel (The Baroness), 39; Journal of, 39.
Ross (Major), 60.
Romans (Bernard), Takes Fort George), 11; Note on, 11; Goes to Albany, 14; Sends expresses, 15.
Rocque (Mary Ann), Plan of Fort George, 5.
Rigaud attacks Fort William Henry, 3.
Sabbath-Day Point, 70, 73.
Shirley (Gen. William), 3.
Stockade, 5, 7.
Sill (Thomas), Killed, 49.
St. Clair (Gen.), a "great soldier, 35, his retreat, 36.
Sherwood (Capt.), Surrendered Fort Ann, 50, 53.
Schaick (Col.), 31, 32.
Schuyler to Washington, 22, 31, 34, 54, 57.
Sparden (John), his Memorial, 18.
Ticonderoga, 2; Winter expedition against, 3; Amherst attacks Ticonderoga, 8; Delays at, 8, 18; in ruins, 18; Reinforced, 20; Plan for attack, 42; Evacuated, 44.
Tryon (Gov.), 8, 13.
Tiars (Adjutant Peter B.), 65.
Tryon (Gov.), 13.
Trumbull (John), 24.
Trumbull (Jonathan), 16.
Vermont, her negotiations with the British, 55; Fear of, 60.
Warner (Samuel), Journal of, 5, 7.
Washington (Gen.), Letter on, 56.
Woedtke (Death of), 26.
Willett (Col.), his success, 60.
Wilkinson (Sickness of), 26; Letter to Gates, 34.
Williams Dr. Thos.), Letter of, 2

FINIS.

www.ingramcontent.com/pod-product-compliance
Lightning Source LLC
Chambersburg PA
CBHW020331090426
42735CB00009B/1488